FC BARCELONA
TRAINING SESSIONS

160 PRACTICES FROM 34 TACTICAL SITUATIONS

WRITTEN BY ATHANASIOS TERZIS

PUBLISHED BY

FC BARCELONA
TRAINING SESSIONS

160 PRACTICES FROM
34 TACTICAL SITUATIONS

First Published August 2013 by SoccerTutor.com

Info@soccertutor.com | www.SoccerTutor.com

UK: 0208 1234 007 | **US:** (305) 767 4443 | **ROTW:** +44 208 1234 007
ISBN: 978-0-9576705-3-2

Author
Athanasios Terzis © 2013

Edited by
Alex Fitzgerald - SoccerTutor.com

Cover Design by
Alex Macrides, Think Out Of The Box Ltd.
Email: design@thinkootb.com Tel: +44 (0) 208 144 3550

Diagrams
Diagram designs by SoccerTutor.com. All the diagrams in this book have been created using SoccerTutor.com Tactics Manager Software available from **www.SoccerTutor.com**

Note: While every effort has been made to ensure the technical accuracy of the content of this book, neither the author nor publishers can accept any responsibility for any injury or loss sustained as a result of the use of this material.

MEET THE AUTHOR

ATHANASIOS TERZIS

- UEFA B coaching licence
- M.S.C. certification in coaching and conditioning.

I played for several teams in Greek professional leagues. At the age of 29 I stopped playing and focused on studying football coaching. I have been head coach of several semi-pro football teams in Greece and worked as a technical director in the Academies of DOXA Dramas (Greek football league, 2nd division).

I wrote and published two books "4-3-3 the application of the system" and "4-4-2 with diamond in midfield, the application of the system". I then decided to proceed in something more specific so coaches would have an idea of how top teams apply the same systems. I published two further books which have become extremely successful and sold thousands worldwide:

1. FC Barcelona: A Tactical Analysis.

2. Jose Mourinho's Real Madrid: A Tactical Analysis.

Analysing games tactically is a great love and strength of mine. I think teams have success only when they prepare well tactically.

I have watched Barcelona in most of their league and Champions league matches for the last seven years and less frequently over the past twenty years. I believe that this Barcelona side is by far the best Barcelona I have ever seen in regards to their attractive style of play and success in becoming the best football side in the world. I have analysed Barcelona's tactics for this book, which together with the teams' incredible technical ability allows Barca to perform their attractive brand of football.

I have now decided to use my tactical analysis to produce ready made sessions for coaches to train their teams the 'Barca way.'

This book contains tactical and technical exercises that have been formulated from the tactical situations which are presented in my previous book *'FC Barcelona: A Tactical Analysis'.*

We analyse deeply how and why Pep Guardiola's Barcelona, possibly the best team of all time, used their specific tactics in different situations.

We provide a training session for each tactical situation with progressive exercises.

We produce a guide for how coaches can train the tactics used by F.C. Barcelona.

My dream is to use my skills at the professional level.

Athanasios Terzis

ATHANASIOS TERZIS in collaboration with:

KONSTANTINOS TERZIS

Konstantinos Terzis has a bachelor degree in Physical Education, specialising in football. He also has a Master Science Certification in Coaching and Conditioning and is a UEFA 'B' licence coach.

He played as a goalkeeper at semi-professional level with teams in Greece. He worked as a head coach for several semi-pro teams in Greece and as an assistant coach for the Doxa Dramas U20 team.

Konstantinos also worked as a fitness coach for Doxa Dramas (Greek 2nd division) and in Fokikos Amfissas (also Greek 2nd division). For the coming season (2013-14), he is now the head coach of Drama W.S (womens team) in the Greek first division.

DIMITRIOS TZOUVARAS

Dimitrios Tzouvaras has a bachelor degree in Physical Education, specialising in football and is a UEFA 'B' licence coach.

He played football for several semi-professional teams in Greece. When he stopped playing, Dimitrios worked as a fitness coach at semi-pro teams. He has also worked as a technical director in several football academies, such as Filotas Florinas and A.O Proteas in Thessaloniki.

During the previous season (2012-13), Dimitrios was the head coach for the Apollon Kalamarias U17 team (Greek 2nd division).

TO MY PARENTS
GIORGOS AND MELPOMENI

COACHING FORMAT

1. Tactical Situation.

2. Full Training Session from the Tactical Situation.

   • Technical / Functional unopposed practices
   • Tactical opposed practices
   • Progressions and variations

KEY

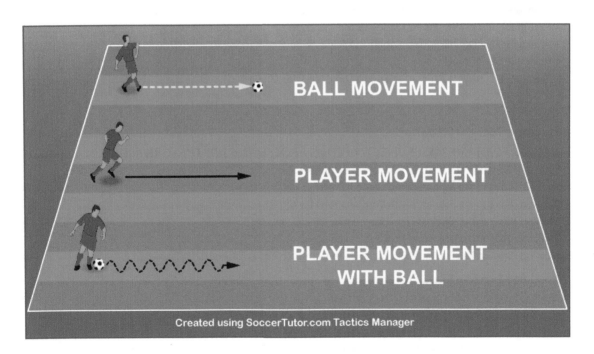

BALL MOVEMENT

PLAYER MOVEMENT

PLAYER MOVEMENT WITH BALL

Created using SoccerTutor.com Tactics Manager

CONTENT

INTRODUCTION

This book contains tactical and technical exercises that have been formulated from the tactical situations which are presented in the book **'FC Barcelona: A Tactical Analysis - Attacking and Defending'**.

This book has 2 main aims:

1. To deeply analyse how and why Pep Guardiola's Barcelona, possibly the best team of all time, used their specific tactics in different situations.

2. Provide a training session for each tactical situation with progressive exercises.

We produce a guide for how coaches can train the tactics used by F.C. Barcelona.

PASSING PRACTICES

15 Passing Exercises on How to Coach Barcelona's Quick Combinations and Unique Attacking Style of Play

ANALYSIS

FCB PASSING COMBINATIONS

On these diagrams there are several passing combinations which were regularly used during Barcelona's attacking play.

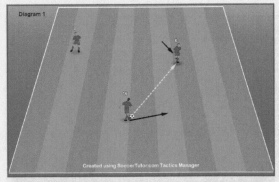

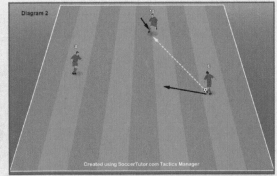

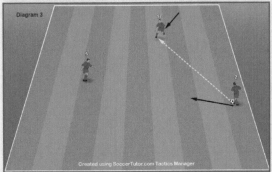

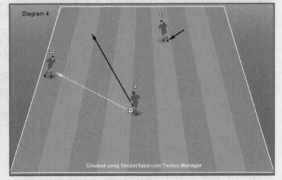

On diagrams 1-3, there are passing combinations which contain passing and moving to receive the back pass from different players in different areas of the pitch.

On diagram 4, there is a pass and a diagonal movement towards the sideline in order for superiority in numbers to be created.

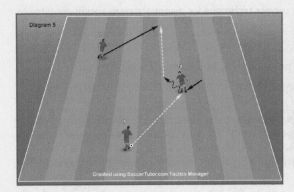

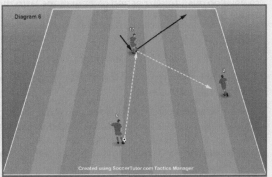

On diagram 5, there is a movement towards the ball carrier, a turn with the first touch and a vertical (final) pass after a forward's diagonal movement.

On diagram 6, there is a combination which contains a movement towards the ball carrier, a back pass and a diagonal movement towards the free space.

PRACTICES FOR THIS TOPIC (15)

1. Technical: One-Two Combinations in a Pass and Move Pattern of Play

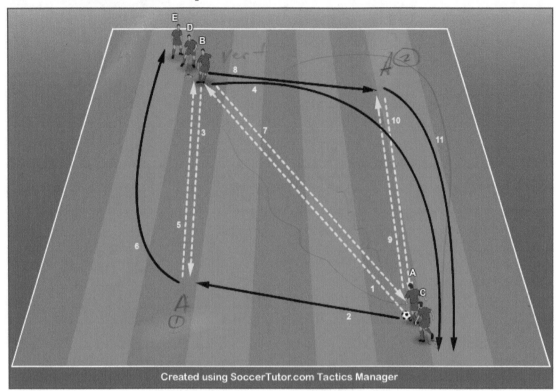

Created using SoccerTutor.com Tactics Manager

Objective

We develop our 1 touch passing combinations, with the proper technique for diagonal passes and moving to receive the pass back.

Description

In an area 20 x 10 yards, 5 players work on this pass and move pattern of play with 1-2 combinations.

Every player who passes diagonally moves to receive the pass back. The players who pass vertically then move directly to the other corner.

Player A passes diagonally to player B and moves to receive the pass back. B passes vertically to A and moves to the opposite corner. A passes to player D (the first player in the row now) and moves to the opposite corner. Player D passes diagonally to player C and moves to receive the pass back. C passes vertically to D and runs to the opposite corner. D passes to B, who has already taken a position on the opposite corner, and the sequence continues. All players are limited to 1 touch.

Coaching Points

1. Focus on the correct technique for diagonal passing and receiving the ball.
2. The timing of the pass to the run is key in this pass and move pattern of play.

2. Technical: One-Two Combinations in a Pass and Move Pattern of Play (2)

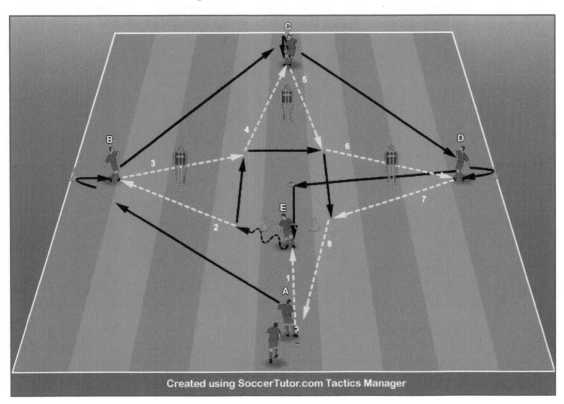

Created using SoccerTutor.com Tactics Manager

Objective

We practice passing combinations, focusing on creating space and moving to receive the ball back from one-two combinations.

Description

In an area 30 x 30 yards, 6 players participate in this practice.

Player A passes to Player E who has run through the 2 cones and then moves to B's position. E turns and passes to Player B behind the mannequin who passes back for E's run (as shown). The players should move towards the cone and touch it before they move to receive and pass back.

This is repeated with player E playing 1-2 combinations with C and D. The last pass (8) is directed to the next player who was waiting behind A and E takes up his position. Player D runs through the cones (as E did the first time) and the same sequence is repeated..

Coaching Point

Focus on the correct technique and quality (timing/weight) of the pass.

3. Pass and Move: Creating Space Pattern of Play (1)

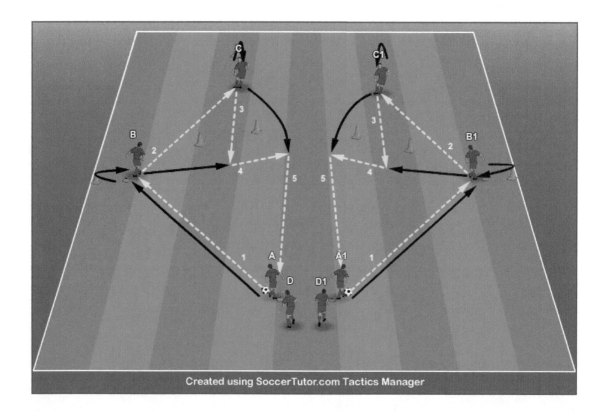

Created using SoccerTutor.com Tactics Manager

Objective

We work on creating space, receiving, passing and the movement to receive the pass back.

Description

In an area 30 x 30 yards, 8 players participate in this passing practice.

Player A and A1 pass to B and B1 respectively, who have moved and touched the traffic cones in order to create space for themselves. B plays the double 1-2 with C (first touch with the left, second with right) and B1 with C1 (first touch with right, second with left). C and C1 also have to make a move to touch the traffic cones before they receive from B and B1.

After the combination between B and C, the balls are passed to D1 and D respectively. A and A1 move quickly to B and B1, B and B1 to C and C1 & C and C1 to the starting point. D and D1 are the players who begin the new sequence of passes.

Coaching Points

1. Synchronisation of the passes to the movements are needed for the practice to flow on both sides at the same time.
2. Focus on the correct technique and quality (timing/weight) of the pass.

4. Pass and Move: Creating Space Pattern of Play (2)

Created using SoccerTutor.com Tactics Manager

Objective

To develop quick passing combinations with the focus on creating space and training the movement to receive the pass. This situation usually occurred near the sidelines for Barcelona.

Description

In an area 20 x 10 yards, we play a quick passing combinations around 4 mannequins (as shown on the diagram).

No.3 passes to 17 who checks away first and passes to No.2. 17 then runs round the red pole as shown and gets ready to get involved again. At the same time, No.7 takes advantage of the space created by 17, receives from No.2 and passes back to him to the other side of the mannequin. No.2 then plays the final pass back to No.3.

No3 starts a new passing sequence towards the left this time with the first pass to No.7 this time, with 17 and 22 combining. After the first pass, 3 and 2 swap positions for the next sequence.

Coaching Points

1. The correct body shape should be monitored (opening up) and receiving/passing with the back foot (foot furthest away from the ball).

2. Synchronisation of the passes to the movements are needed for the practice to flow on both sides at the same time.

5. Turn, Pass and Move Pattern of Play

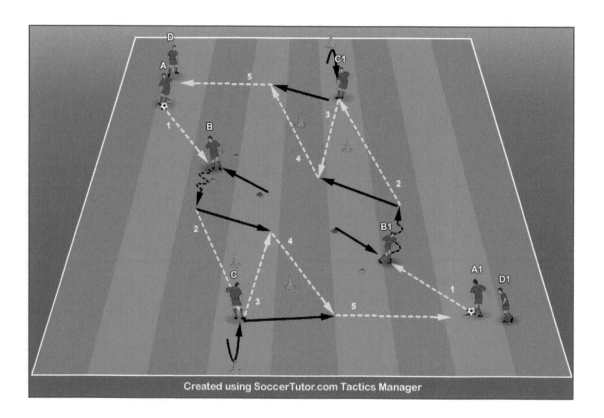

Created using SoccerTutor.com Tactics Manager

Objective

We practice the technical elements to turn, pass and move.

Description

In an area 30 x 30 yards, we play a turn, move and pass pattern of play.

Player A and A1 pass to B and B1 respectively as soon as they have moved through the 2 red cones.

They receive on the half turn and play their pass to C/C1. These players have already made a movement to touch the traffic cones before moving towards the passing lane.

They then play the double 1-2 with C/C1 and the final passes are played to D/D1. All players move into the next position (A to B, B to C and C to D). The sequence starts again with D and D1.

Coaching Points

1. Ensure quality in the turning and the passing.
2. Accuracy of pass, weight of pass and good communication are all key elements for this practice.
3. There needs to be rhythm and timing of the movement together with the pass.

6. One Touch Combination Play with an Overlapping Run

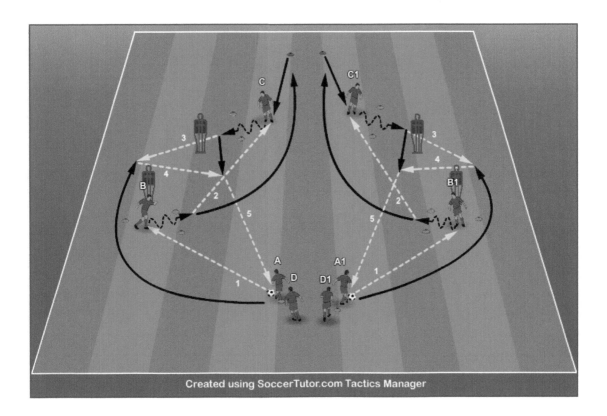

Created using SoccerTutor.com Tactics Manager

Objective
To develop the first touch and combination play.

Description
In an area 30 x 30 yards, this practice is used to improve the first touch and combination play after an overlapping run.

Player A and A1 pass to B and B1 respectively and then make the overlapping run (as shown).

B and B1 receive with a directional first touch inside and in between the 2 cones (B with the left foot and B1 with the right) in order to move away from their maker (mannequin). Then they pass to players C and C1 who drop back at the right moment and move to receive the pass.

C and C1 take a first touch towards the outside (C with the left foot, C1 with the right) and pass to players A and A1 who have made the overlap and receive the first time pass. Then they pass towards the starting point. All players move to the next position (A to B, B to C, C to D). Players D and D1 start the sequence again.

Coaching Points
1. The accuracy and weight of pass needs to be correct.
2. The players need to take good directional first touches to dribble round the mannequins.

7. Taking Advantage of Space in a One Touch Pattern of Play

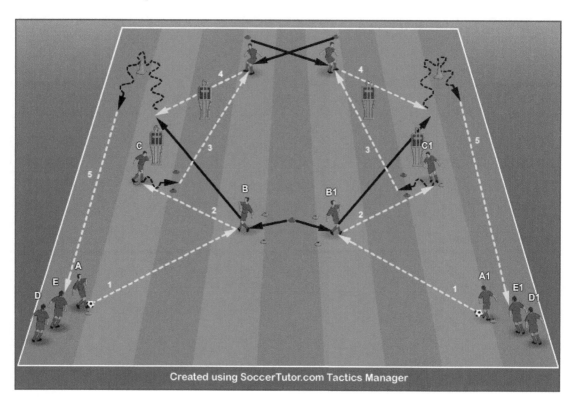

Created using SoccerTutor.com Tactics Manager

Objective

To develop the first touch, together with passing and moving.

Description

In an area 40 x 40 yards, this practice works on improving the first touch together with passing and moving towards the free space in a pattern of play.

Players A and A1 pass to B and B1 respectively (as soon as they have run through the 2 cones). B and B1 pass to players C and C1 and move towards the free space behind the mannequins. The new players in possession take a directional first touch in the opposite direction (inside) and through the blue cones (C with the left foot, C1 with the right) and pass to the forwards who move at the right moment to provide support from the opposite side and pass to B and B1.

B and B1 receive the pass, dribble the ball around the cone and pass it to the starting position (E/E1). A and A1 move to B and B1, B and B1 to C and C1, and C and C1 behind players D and D1.

Coaching Points

1. The accuracy and weight of pass needs to be correct.
2. Make sure the players communicate with their teammates and heads are up.

8. Technical: One Touch Passing

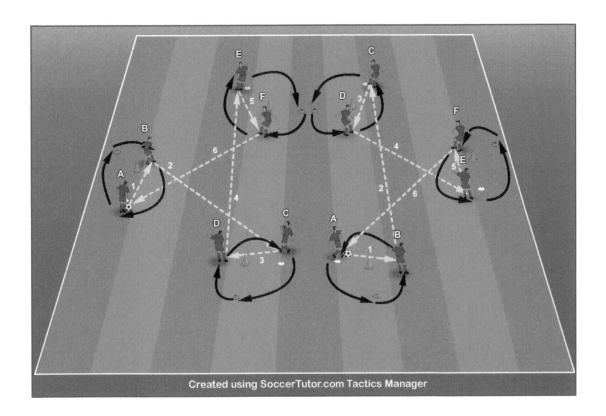

Created using SoccerTutor.com Tactics Manager

Objective

To develop the technique for one touch passing.

Description

In an area 30 x 30 yards, we practice one touch play. The players work in pairs. The passes from one pair to another are directed towards the players on the small white cones.

Player A begins by setting up B with a pass in front of him. B makes a movement in front of the red traffic cone to receive and pass to C who sets up for D. D passes to E, who sets up for F who passes back to the starting point (Player A). The sequence is then repeated again.

The drill is executed with both sides running at the same time. All players switch positions with their partner after each contact with the ball. The players on the left usually pass with their left foot, while the players who work in the drill on the right side usually pass with their right.

Coaching Points

1. The correct body shape should be monitored (opening up) and passing with the back foot.
2. When setting up a pass it needs to be out in front of the receiver to be able to pass first time.
3. The rhythm and timing of the movement together with the pass is key.

9. First Touch and Awareness Passing Sequence (1)

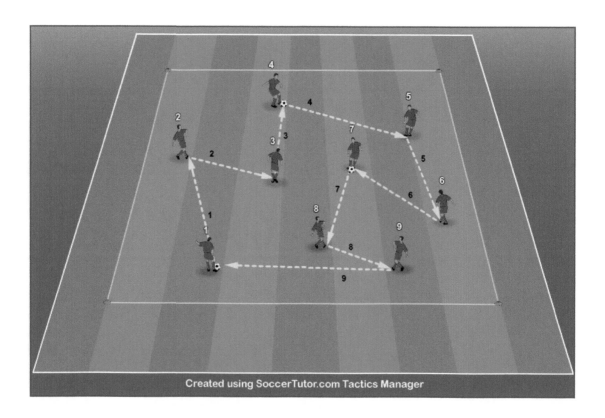

Created using SoccerTutor.com Tactics Manager

Objective

To develop awareness, keeping the first touch close to the feet and using the correct body shape.

Description

In an area 25 x 25 yards, 9 players inside the marked area are numbered from 1 to 9. We play with 3 balls, with Players 1, 4 and 7 starting in possession. The players should pass the ball in number sequence. They receive from the player with the previous number and pass to the player with the next number. With 3 balls in play they need to be quickly ready to receive after playing their pass.

The players use 2 touches (receive and pass). The first touch is made close to the players' feet in order to prepare for a quick and accurate pass. Limit to 1 touch for more advanced players.

Variation

Use more or fewer balls depending on the age/level of the players.

Coaching Point

The players should be constantly moving and changing their body shape to be aware of who they are going to receive from, as well as to who they are going to pass the ball to.

10. First Touch and Awareness Passing Sequence (2)

Created using SoccerTutor.com Tactics Manager

Objective

To develop awareness of free space and directional first touches into free space.

Description

Using the same area, we have a variation of the previous drill. The difference is that now the first touch is made towards the player who is to receive the next pass.

The player about to receive represents the free space for the ball carrier. After playing a pass, the players should sprint for a few yards before moving to receive the next pass. The players are limited to 2 touches.

Coaching Points

1. Players need to use a well weighted directional first touch to maintain the flow of the practice and speed up play.

2. The players should be constantly moving.

3. Awareness of the player receiver (space) before receiving the ball and the server should be maintained at all times.

11. Overcoming the Opposition's Pressure Possession Game

Created using SoccerTutor.com Tactics Manager

Objective

To develop possession play, working on overcoming the pressure from the opposition to retain the ball.

Description

In an area 20 x 20 yards, 2 teams play a 7v3 possession game. The 5 red players take up positions outside the playing area while their 2 teammates are positioned inside. The red players (attackers) seek to retain possession with the help of the 2 inside players while the white ones (defenders) try to win the ball.

The red players inside the marked area move towards the available passing lanes and help their teammates to overcome the opposition's pressure and retain the ball. The outside players can move from side to side. The player that loses possession swaps roles with one of the defenders. Limit the players to 1 touch.

Variation

The drill can be executed with more or less balls according to the age/level of the players.

Coaching Points

1. The correct body shape should be monitored (opening up) and receiving/passing with the back foot (foot furthest away from the ball).
2. Players should be constantly moving, trying to find the available passing lanes.

12. First Touch and Awareness Possession Game

Created using SoccerTutor.com Tactics Manager

Objective

To develop the first touch and awareness of available space.

Description

In an area 20 x 20 yards, we have 2 teams playing a 7v3 possession game. The 5 red players take up positions outside the playing area, with 2 of their teammates positioned inside.

The red players (attackers) seek to retain possession with the help of the 2 inside players while the white players (defenders) try to win the ball.

The inside players must use 2 touches, so they have to be aware of the available space in order to make their first touch towards this space. The outside players are limited to 1 touch. The player that loses possession swaps roles with one of the defenders.

Coaching Points

1. Players should be constantly moving, trying to find the available passing lanes.
2. Players need to take advantage of the free space created by the numerical advantage.

13. Switching Play 'Double Square' Possession Game

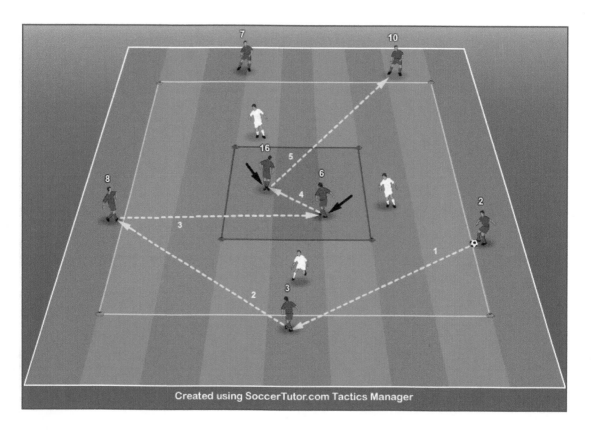

Created using SoccerTutor.com Tactics Manager

Objective

We practice retaining possession and switching play (changing the direction).

Description

In an area 25 x 25 yards, 2 teams play 7v3. 5 red players take up positions outside the playing area while their 2 teammates are positioned inside the blue square area.

The red players (attackers) seek to retain possession and find a way to pass the ball to the players inside the blue area. If there is no passing angle available (due to an opponent's pressure) they should search for the free side as there will always be a player free.

To score a point, they must complete 10 or 15 consecutive passes or pass the ball 2 or 3 times (depending on the level of the players) to the players inside and these players successfully switch the play. The outside players can move along the side they are positioned on.

The whites are not allowed to enter the blue square. The red players are limited to 1 touch and both the inside players should have at least one touch before they can pass outside again.

Coaching Points

1. Players need to have good vision and awareness of the available free side.
2. Players should be constantly moving, trying to find the available passing lanes.

14. Using the Correct Body Shape in a 5v5 (+1) Possession Game

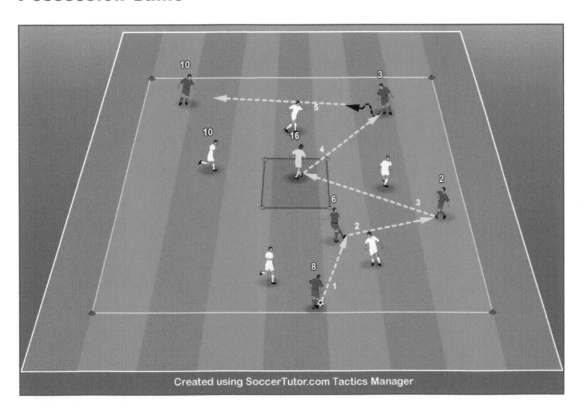

Created using SoccerTutor.com Tactics Manager

Objective

To develop the correct body shape to determine the next pass and retaining possession.

Description

In an area 30 x 30 yards, 2 teams play a 5v5 possession game with a neutral player positioned in a central zone.

The neutral player plays with the team in possession to help them retain the ball. The neutral player can only use 1 touch and thus has to use the appropriate body shape in order to pass successfully.

The rest of the players are limited to 2 touches. The teams win a point when they manage to complete 10 consecutive passes.

Coaching Points

1. The neutral player needs to be aware of the available passing options before receiving the ball.

2. This practice needs a high quality of passing (well weighted and timed).

3. The players should be constantly moving to create space or move to receive a pass.

15. Forming the Correct Shapes in an End to End Possession Game

Objective

We work on moving the ball from end to end by forming the correct shapes and retaining possession.

Description

The teams play 4 (+ 4 neutrals) v 4 inside a 25 x 35 yards area. The 2 teams inside the area want to retain possession and move the ball from the neutral players on one side to the ones on the other side (1 point). However, the players inside have to complete at least 2 passes before they can pass to the neutrals on the other side.

The players in possession try to form the correct shapes (rhombus and triangles) in order for the neutral player in possession to have available passing options and make retaining possession easier.

The players inside can pass the ball back to the neutral player who they received from in order to avoid losing possession.

The outside players have 1 touch or they have to pass within 3 seconds (depending on the level of the players). If the outside player takes longer than 3 seconds, the coach passes a ball to the opposite team and the game goes on with them in possession.

Coaching Point

The correct body shape should be monitored (opening up) and receiving/passing with the back foot (furthest away from the ball).

ATTACKING

ATTACKING TACTICAL SITUATION 1

Forward Passes Directly from the Defenders to the Forwards

ANALYSIS

FORWARD PASSES DIRECTLY FROM THE DEFENDERS TO THE FORWARDS

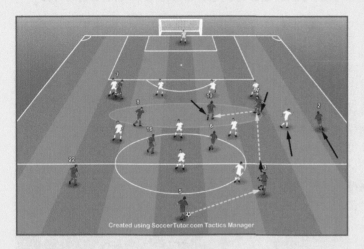

Situation 1

The centre back takes advantage of the free space ahead of him and moves forward with the ball.

The winger (17) drops back into a passing lane and becomes the link player as No.10 (Messi) receives the ball through him inside the available space behind the opposition's midfield line.

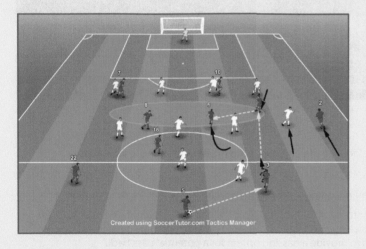

Situation 2

In this second situation, instead of No.10, this time No.6 (Xavi) makes the well timed forward run and receives the pass from No.17 behind the 4 white midfielders and is facing the opposition's goal.

Analysis

Receiving a pass inside the area behind the opposition's midfielders with a body position that allows the player to face the opposition's goal could easily lead to a final pass.

In order for this objective to be achieved, the forwards and sometimes the attacking midfielders moved to potential passing lanes when the defender in possession had available space in front of him.

If the pass was directed to them they could be link players in order for the ball to be passed to another forward or to a forward moving attacking midfielder facing the opposition's goal.

SESSION FOR THIS TACTICAL SITUATION
(5 PRACTICES)
1. Passing Direct to the Forwards with Combination Play

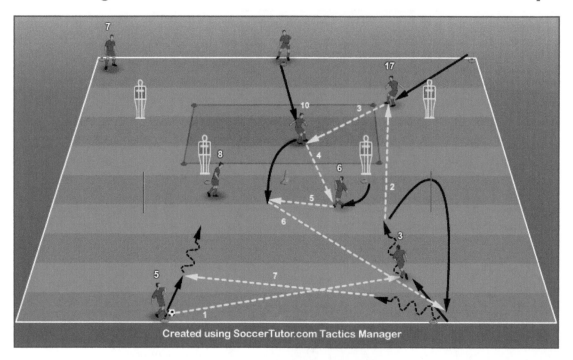

Created using SoccerTutor.com Tactics Manager

Objective

We practice passing combinations with a focus on direct passes from the defenders to the forwards.

Description

We use an area 30 x 30 yards and have 4 mannequins, 2 poles, a marked out rectangle area and a traffic cone.

The centre back (5) passes to the other centre back (3), who receives the ball and dribbles forward. As soon as he receives, both the winger (17) and the attacking midfielder (6) move to provide potential passing options. No.3 passes forwards to the winger and moves to provide a passing option for a potential pass back.

At the same time, the centre forward (10) drops back inside the target area behind the 2 mannequins (which replicate the positions of opposition midfield players), receives and combines with the attacking midfielder. The final pass is back to No.3 who has run round the pole into his starting position. No.3 receives and passes towards the other centre back (5) and the drill starts again towards the left side.

Coaching Points

1. The defenders should move forward quickly with the ball.

2. The accuracy, weight and timing of the passes should be monitored.

3. Players time their movements to receive and use the correct body shape to provide the appropriate passing options.

VARIATION

2. Passing Direct to the Forwards with Combination Play (2)

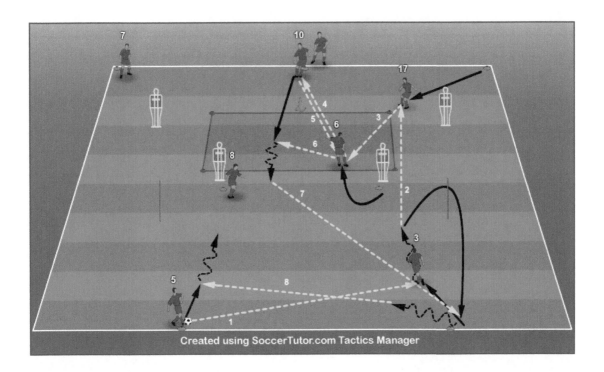

Created using SoccerTutor.com Tactics Manager

Objective

We practice passing combinations with a focus on forward passes from the defenders to the forwards.

Description

Here we have a variation of the previous drill using the same size area.

The centre back(5) passes to the other centre back (3), who receives the ball and dribbles forward. As soon as he receives, both the winger (17) and the attacking midfielder (6) move to provide potential passing options. No.3 passes forwards to the winger and moves to provide a passing option for a potential pass back.

At the same time, No.6 moves forward into the target area, receives and combines with No.10. The final pass is back to No.3 who has run round the pole into his starting position. No.3 receives and passes towards the other centre back (5) and the drill starts again towards the left side.

Coaching Points

1. The defenders should move forward quickly with the ball.

2. The accuracy, weight and timing of the passes should be monitored.

3. Players time their movements to receive and use the correct body shape to provide the appropriate passing options.

PROGRESSION

3. Passing Through the Midfield Line 3 Zone Possession Game

Created using SoccerTutor.com Tactics Manager

Objective

We practice passing combinations with a focus on passing through the midfield line.

Description

In an area 40 x 45 yards with two 20 x 20 yard zones and a 5 x 20 yards central zone, 2 teams play 3v3 inside both end zones and seek to retain possession and complete at least 4 consecutive passes with the help of the neutral players who are positioned inside the central area with 4 mannequins. If they complete 4 passes, they can then pass the ball to one of their teammates on the other side through the passing lanes (between the mannequins).

When receiving a pass from the opposite side, a player should use 1 touch to pass the ball to a neutral player. After this pass, their team will try to complete 4 passes and then pass back to the opposite side again. The coach passes a new ball in every time the ball goes out of play.

The neutrals inside the blue area are limited to 1 touch as are the rest of the players when receiving the vertical pass from one area to another.

Coaching Points

1. The focus is on intelligent movement towards the available passing lanes and providing available passing options.

2. The quality passes need to be synchronised to the well timed movements to receive.

PROGRESSION

4. Building Up From the Back in a 3 Zone Dynamic SSG

Created using SoccerTutor.com Tactics Manager

Objective

We practice passing combinations with a focus on direct passes from the defenders to the forwards.

Description

In an area 40 x 60 yards, 2 teams play a 10v9 game. Inside the high zone there is a 3v3 situation, inside the middle zone there is a 3v3 situation and inside the low zone there is a 3v2 situation.

The red team's defenders aim to pass the ball to the forwards inside the high zone with the help of the 3 midfielders (skipping the middle one). The red midfielders inside the blue area seek to receive the passes back from the forwards and then with the help of their teammates, try to score a goal.

The red players inside the blue area act as neutrals and help the defenders retain possession but they are not allowed to pass the ball directly to the forwards.

The 3 white players inside the middle area try to intercept the passes. As soon as the pass towards the forwards has been made, there are no restrictions in regards to the zones and the players move freely. If the white players win the ball while defending, there are no restrictions for them either as they launch a counter attack and try to score.

During the first stage, the red players in the blue zone are limited to 1 touch, while the red players inside the low zone play freely. The forwards are limited to 1 touch when receiving the vertical pass.

Coaching Points

1. The focus is on intelligent movement towards the available passing lanes.
2. The players provide available passing options with intelligent synchronised movements.

PROGRESSION

5. Passing Direct to The Forwards 'Receiving Zone' Game

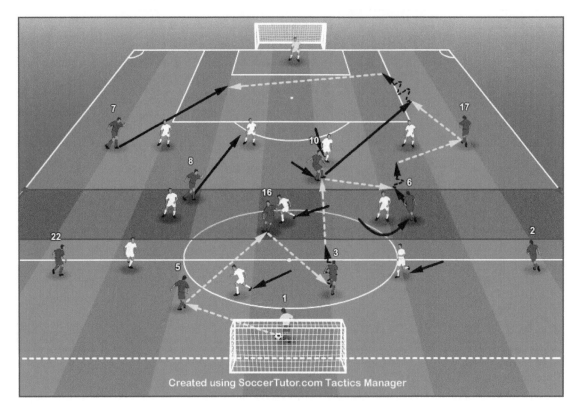

Created using SoccerTutor.com Tactics Manager

Objective

We practice passing combinations with a focus on direct passes from the defenders to the forwards.

Description

We now use 2/3 of a full pitch and 2 teams play an 11v11 game. There is a 4v3 situation in the low zone, a 3v3 inside the middle zone and a 4v3 inside the high zone. The red defenders inside the low zone aim to pass the ball directly to the forwards inside the high zone so the team can move to the 3rd stage of the attacking phase quickly.

The 3 midfielders inside the middle zone (blue area) help the defenders find the passing lanes towards the forwards but they cannot pass the ball forward themselves. As soon as the forwards receive the ball, there are no restrictions in moving from area to area. The restrictions are also removed when the white players win the ball.

The forwards are limited to 1 touch when receiving the vertical passes. The midfielders are also limited to 1 touch when helping the defenders find passing lanes.

Coaching Points

1. The defenders need to display good vision, awareness and timing to find the right pass through the midfield line (available passing options).
2. The forwards should check away from their marker before moving to receive the ball.

ATTACKING TACTICAL SITUATION 2

Defenders Joining the Midfield

ANALYSIS

DEFENDERS JOINING THE MIDFIELD

Created using SoccerTutor.com Tactics Manager

Analysis

Barcelona used their defenders' abilities to run with the ball out from the back (especially Pique) in order to create a numerical superiority in midfield.

Specifically, Pique here in this example (3) receives and moves forward with the ball and reaches the midfield zone.

Superiority in numbers is created around the ball as there is a 4v3 situation in favour of Barcelona.

Barcelona take advantage of this and move the ball to the free player, Daniel Alves (2).

40

SESSION FOR THIS TACTICAL SITUATION
(4 PRACTICES)
1. Running With the Ball Out from the Back

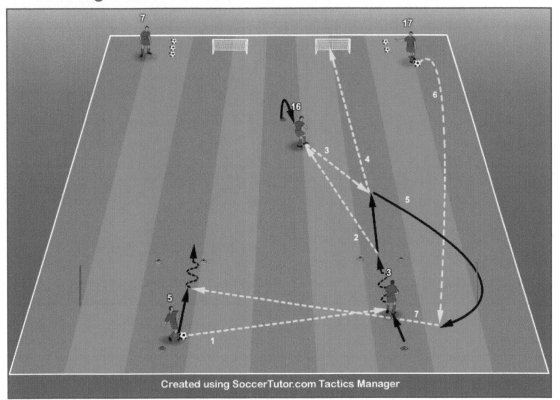

Created using SoccerTutor.com Tactics Manager

Objective

We train the defenders to play out from the back and dribble forward with the ball to create a numerical advantage in midfield.

Description

In an area 40 x 30 yards, 5 players participate in this practice which should be executed at a high tempo and is about moving forward with the ball, passing with accuracy and receiving on the move.

The centre back (5) passes to the other centre back (3). The new man in possession dribbles the ball forward between the 2 red cones and plays a 1-2 combination with the defensive midfielder.

The defender then must make an accurate pass into the small goal, sprint round the pole (as shown in the diagram), receive the long ball from No.17 and pass to the other centre back. After this last pass, the drill is then executed on the left.

Coaching Points

1. The centre back should display good quality when dribbling the ball forward quickly, keeping the ball close to his feet.

2. Monitor the correct technique for receiving and passing the ball in the air.

PROGRESSION

2. Defenders Joining the Midfield in a 3v3 (+4) Possession Game

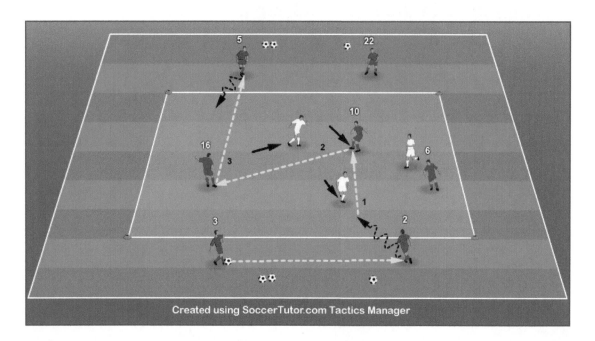

Created using SoccerTutor.com Tactics Manager

Objective

We work on the defenders joining the midfield in order to create superiority in numbers and help move the ball forward.

Description

We mark out an area 20 x 30 yards with a 3v3 situation inside. The neutral players outside the area are the team's 4 defenders and the inside players are the midfielders.

The game starts when one of the defenders dribbling the ball inside aiming to combine with the team that passed him the ball (blue in the diagram) in order to find a way to pass the ball to the free player and then towards the defenders on the opposite side. That neutral player returns to his position outside. The neutral who is now in possession does the same.

If the white team win possession, they play against the 3 blue players and seek to complete 2 passes before passing the ball to one of the neutral players themselves. Then the neutrals (defenders) seek to combine with the white players instead of the blue and help to move the ball to the other side again. The neutral players can pass the ball to each other outside using 1 touch before one of them decides to enter the area.

Coaching Points

1. The defenders need to display quality as they dribble the ball quickly forwards to create a numerical advantage in the area.

2. Midfielders should check away from their marker before moving to receive (creating space and passing options).

PROGRESSION

3. Creating a Numerical Advantage in Midfield & Finishing Practice

Created using SoccerTutor.com Tactics Manager

Objective

We work on the defenders joining the midfield in order to create superiority in numbers and help move the ball forward.

Description

In an area 30 x 40 yards, there is a 4v4 situation inside the marked area which becomes 5v4 as soon as one of the defenders enters.

The game starts with the coach passing to the defenders outside the area. They can enter the playing area immediately or can pass (using 1 touch) to each other waiting for the right moment. The attacking team (blue) aim to take advantage of the extra man in order to find a way to dribble the ball through the end line and shoot on goal unopposed.

If the defending team win the ball, they try to pass the ball to the coach inside the blue area. If they succeed, they become the attacking team. When this happens, the defender who was inside the area takes up his starting position and the game starts again with the team's roles reversed.

However, if the blues win the ball back before the whites manage to pass to the coach, they should also pass the ball back to the coach in order for the game to start again.

Coaching Points

1. We create a numerical advantage, so there should always be 1 free player available in the area.
2. Midfielders should check away from their marker before moving to receive.

PROGRESSION

4. Creating a Numerical Advantage in Midfield in a 3 Zone SSG

Created using SoccerTutor.com Tactics Manager

Objective

We work on the defenders joining the midfield in order to create superiority in numbers and help move the ball forward during an attack on the right.

Description

In this 11v11 game, we use 2/3 of a full pitch with 2 equally big end zones and a smaller central zone.

There is a 4v3 in favour of the defenders inside the end zones and a 3v3 inside the central zone. 1 red defender looks to move forward with the ball into the blue area to create a numerical advantage. Then the red team combine with each other inside the blue area (and with the forwards) in order to create space for the free player to receive the ball and dribble into the high zone.

We then have a 4v4 in the high zone with the red team trying to score. The white players try to win the ball and counter attack. As soon as the whites win possession, the restrictions are removed in regards to the zones. If the ball goes out of play, the game starts with the red goalkeeper and the players all move back to their starting positions.

Coaching Points

1. The defender/midfielder moving forward out of their zone is key to creating a numerical advantage, so there is 1 free player to pass to and move forward.

2. The team should retain their cohesion and balance so they are prepared for the negative transition.

ATTACKING TACTICAL SITUATION 3

Switching Positions During Build Up Play

ANALYSIS

SWITCHING POSITIONS DURING BUILD UP PLAY

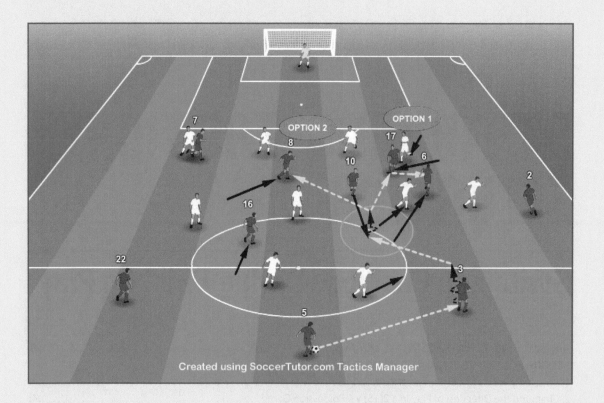

Created using SoccerTutor.com Tactics Manager

Analysis

The switching of positions between the forwards and the midfielders was used in order to create and take advantage of free space deeper in the pitch. So the forwards, after switching positions with the midfielders, could receive, turn and face the opposition's goal.

In this example, No.3 (Pique) receives and moves forward as he has available space before the opposition's forward manages to close him down.

No.6 takes advantage of the situation and makes a movement towards the sideline. This movement forces the opposition's midfielder to follow him in order to prevent a possible numerical advantage for Barcelona on the right side. This creates available space deeper which No.10 drops back to take advantage of, receives unmarked and turns towards the opposition's goal without pressure.

In addition, as soon as No.10 (Messi) receives and turns, the rest of the players move to provide passing options (No.8 and No.17 in the diagram). In this situation, No.17 becomes the link player in order to pass the ball to No.6 (Xavi) who is free of marking in an advanced position.

SESSION FOR THIS TACTICAL SITUATION
(4 PRACTICES)
1. Switching Positions Combination Play

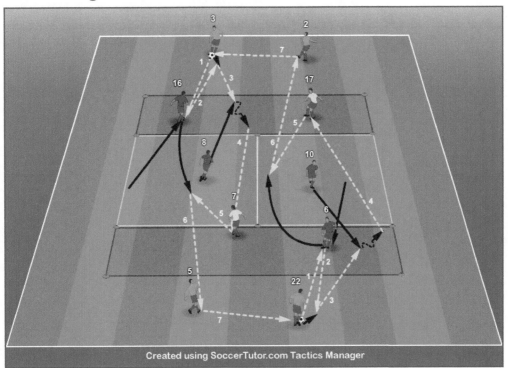

Created using SoccerTutor.com Tactics Manager

Objective

We work on attacking combinations with the focus on switching positions.

Description

4 green players are positioned outside the marked areas and 2 yellow players are positioned inside the red end zones, who do not move from their area. Inside the 2 central zones, there are 2 pairs of red players. The drill is executed with 2 balls, with 1 ball on each side.

The drill starts with No.22 and No.3 respectively. These players pass to the players who drop back into the red area (6 & 16 in the diagram). These players pass back and move into the central zone. As soon as they move forward, No.10 and No.8 drop back into the red end zones, receive on the turn and pass to No.17 and No.7. These players pass using 1 touch to No.6 and No.8 and the ball ends up in No.5 and No.2's possession. They pass to the players beside them and the drill continues.

The pattern is dropping into the red end zone, passing back and moving forward to receive the pass from the link player (yellow). The players should switch roles to participate in all parts of the exercise.

Coaching Points

1. The weight of the pass needs to be synchronised with well timed runs.
2. Monitor the correct technique for quality turns and passes.

PROGRESSION

2. Changing the Direction of Play in a 2(+5) v 4 Possession Game

Created using SoccerTutor.com Tactics Manager

Objective

We work on changing the direction of play with the focus on switching positions.

Description

There is a 2v4 situation inside the 25 x 25 yard area. The 2 red players seek to retain possession using their 5 teammates outside of the area, while the whites try to defend and win the ball.

The 2 red players inside the red zone can drop back one at a time and provide available passing options for their teammates and help them to retain possession. The other 3 outside players can only move along their side and are not allowed to enter the area.

The red player's aim is to complete 15-20 consecutive passes (1 point). If the white team win possession, they play a 4v3 inside the area and aim to complete 5 consecutive passes (1 point).

All the red players are limited to 2 touches. The whites play without limitations.

Coaching Points

1. The players need to have well synchronised movements when switching positions.
2. The players should be constantly moving, using well timed runs and quality passing.

PROGRESSION

3. Switching Positions End Zone Game

Created using SoccerTutor.com Tactics Manager

Objective

We work on the forwards dropping deep.

Description

In an area 45 x 35 yards, the pitch is divided into 2 main zones (high & low) and 1 end zone (10 x 35 yards). The 2 teams play 3v3 (+1 outside) inside the low zone and inside the high zone there is a 3v3 situation. Only 1 red player from the low zone can enter the high zone and only 1 player from the high zone can drop back into the low zone to receive and move forward with the ball.

The red team retain possession inside the low zone and move the ball into the high zone after a switch of positions. The main objective is to reach the end zone (either by dribbling the ball or by receiving a pass inside it). The first pass into the high zone should be by a player who drops back into the low zone (with a switch of positions), receives and moves inside the high zone with a new 4v3 situation. The whites aim to win the ball and dribble the ball through the end red line.

The white players are not allowed to move from area to area unless they win possession. If the switch of positions is not successful, the red players go back to their areas and search for another opportunity. The offside rule is applied throughout the practice.

Coaching Points

1. When dropping back to receive, the player should receive on the half turn to quickly move forward.

2. The players need to have well synchronised movements when switching positions.

3. The forwards should provide passing options as soon as the player dropping deep receives the ball.

PROGRESSION

4. Dropping Deep to Create Space in a 2 Zone SSG

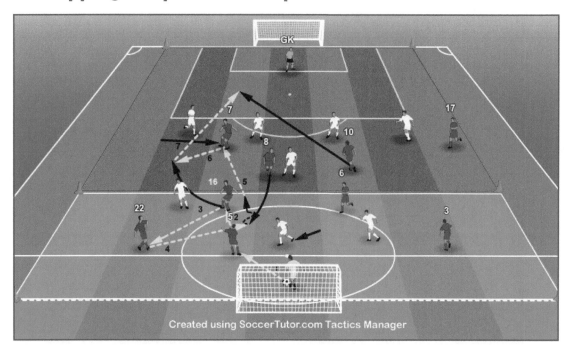

Created using SoccerTutor.com Tactics Manager

Objective

We practice dropping deep to create space with a focus on switching positions.

Description

We play a 10v9 game. We have a 5v3 inside the white area (25 x 45 yards), and we have a 4v5 situation in the blue area (30 x 45 yards).

Only 1 red player from the low zone (white) can enter the high zone (red). Only 1 player from the high zone can drop back into the white zone, receive and move forward with the ball.

The red players inside the low zone aim to retain possession and then move the ball into the high zone after switching positions to create a 5v5 situation. The ball should be moved into the high zone by a red player dropping back from the high zone at the right moment to receive. This player drops back, and either passes the ball or moves forward with the ball into the high zone. The red team tries to score, while the whites try to win possession and launch a counter attack.

The whites are not allowed to move from area to area until they win possession. The reds should switch positions in order to move the ball forward. If the switch of positions is not successful, the players go back to their areas and search for another opportunity.

Coaching Points

1. When dropping back to receive, the player should receive on the half turn to quickly move forward.
2. The players need to have well synchronised movements when switching positions.
3. The forwards should provide passing options as soon as the player dropping deep receives the ball.

ATTACKING TACTICAL SITUATION 4

The Forward Dropping Deep to Maintain Possession

ANALYSIS

THE FORWARD DROPPING DEEP TO MAINTAIN POSSESSION

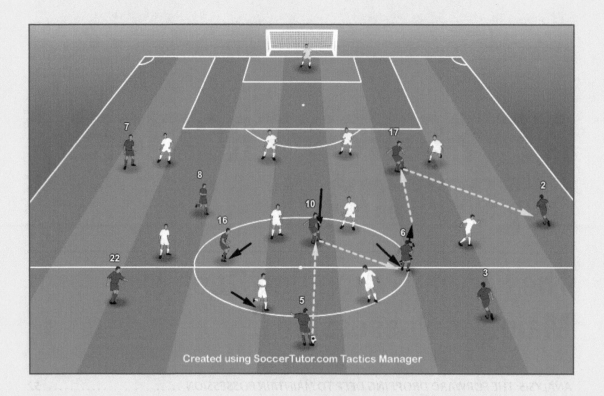

Created using SoccerTutor.com Tactics Manager

Analysis

There were times during Barcelona's attacking phase when the forwards would drop deep to create a numerical advantage in the midfield. This resulted in an extra passing option for the player in possession and helped the team to retain possession.

The players dropping deep were often used as link players in order to work the ball to players who had the passing lanes towards them blocked initially.

In this example, the man in possession (5) is being put under pressure. Additionally the passes towards No.16 and No.6 have been blocked by the 2 white attackers.

The forward (Messi - 10) drops back at the right moment to provide an extra passing option and becomes the link player for the ball to be passed to one of the midfielders.

SESSION FOR THIS TACTICAL SITUATION
(4 PRACTICES)
1. Dropping Deep and Retaining Possession in Midfield

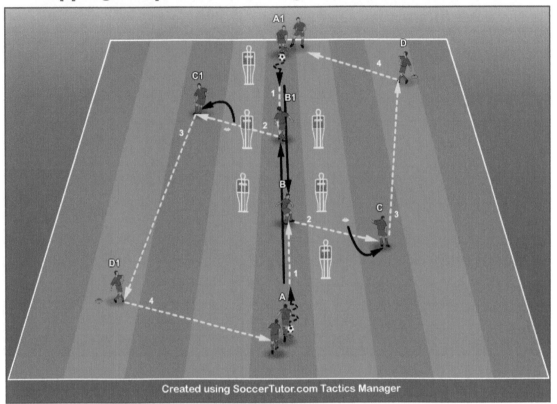

Created using SoccerTutor.com Tactics Manager

Objective

We train the forwards to drop deep to create superiority in numbers and help retain possession in midfield.

Description

In an area 30 x 40 yards, this drill starts with player A and player A1 with a ball each. They move forward with the ball while players B and B1 move towards them and players C and C1 open up to provide an available passing option (making sure to use the correct body shape).

As soon as players B and B1 drop deeper than the 2 mannequins, they receive the passes from A and A1 and pass to C and C1 respectively. C and C1 pass to D and D1 and they pass the ball to the starting positions.

While the other players have been combining, A and A1 time their runs towards the opposite side in order to drop deeper than the 2 mannequins at the right moment to receive. They then repeat the same sequence of passes. Just like A and A1, all the players move to the next position (B to C, C to D, D to the start).

Coaching Points

1. The player dropping deep should use the correct body position to allow a first time pass.

2. The passes and movements (especially dropping back to receive) need to be well synchronised.

PROGRESSION

2. Forwards Dropping Deep Possession Game

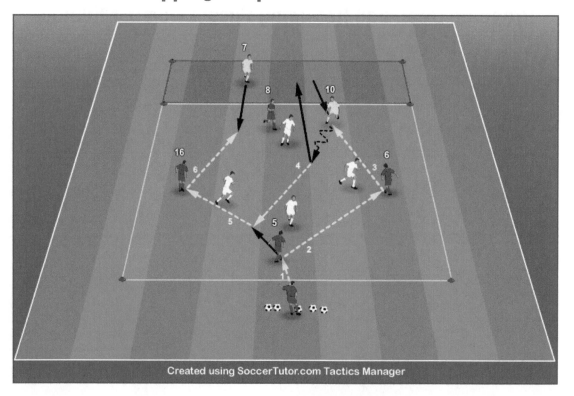

Created using SoccerTutor.com Tactics Manager

Objective

We train the forwards to drop deep to create superiority in numbers and help retain possession in midfield.

Description

In this practice, we have a main area (30 x 30 yards) and an extra zone at the end (5 x 30 yards). The red team aims to retain possession and complete 10 consecutive passes with the help of the forwards (neutral yellow players) and the 1 outside player who plays with 1 touch.

The neutral players drop deep into the main area 1 at a time to provide superiority in numbers and an extra passing option. As soon as the neutral receives and passes the ball, he should move back out of the playing area.

If the whites win the ball, they play 4 (+ 1 neutral) inside against the 4 reds with the aim to complete 5-8 consecutive passes. The number of passes should be relevant to the age/level of the players.

Coaching Point

The neutrals can only stay inside the main area for 5 seconds, so they have to use well timed runs.

PROGRESSION

3. Dropping Deep with Quick Break Attacks in a 3 Zone SSG

Objective

We train the forwards to drop deep to create superiority in numbers and help retain possession in midfield, with quick break attacks.

Description

In an area 60 x 40 yards, 2 teams play 5v5 inside the low zone and there is 1 white defender and a goalkeeper in the opposite zone. The red team's forward is inside the middle red area and can enter the low zone in order to receive and pass the ball to help his teammates retain possession.

The red team has to complete at least 3-4 passes (or more for a higher level) with the forward touching the ball at least once. They are then allowed to pass the ball forward into the other zones. If they manage to do this, they try to score past the goalkeeper. If the whites win the ball, they can score in 1 of the 2 small goals without any limitations/restrictions.

The red forward can stay in the white area for 5 seconds. If he does not receive within this time, he has to go back into the middle zone. The offside rule is applied in case the players enter the high zone before the pass in made. After the pass is made into the high zone, all the players can then move forward freely.

PROGRESSION

4. Dropping Deep with Quick Break Attacks 11v11 Game

Created using SoccerTutor.com Tactics Manager

Objective

We train the forwards to drop deep to create superiority in numbers and help retain possession in midfield.

Description

Using 2/3 of a full pitch, 2 teams play 6v6 inside the low zone (white) and 4v4 inside the high zone.

All players move within their area except 1 red player who can drop back into the low zone (to create a numerical advantage) and help his teammates retain possession and move the ball forward. The red team's aim is to complete at least 4-6 consecutive passes (or more) in order to be able to then move the ball into the high zone.

During this sequence, the player who drops deep must touch the ball at least once. As soon as the ball is passed into the high zone, all players can then move forward into it. If the whites win the ball, they look to score without any limitations/restrictions.

The 4 white defenders are not allowed to enter the low zone unless their team wins possession.

Coaching Points

1. The forwards need to use timed runs when dropping inside the white zone (displaying intelligence and awareness to select the right moment).

2. The players should be constantly moving, always trying to create available passing options.

ATTACKING TACTICAL SITUATION 5

Creating Space for Others to Exploit in the Low Zone

ANALYSIS

CREATING SPACE FOR OTHERS TO EXPLOIT IN THE LOW ZONE

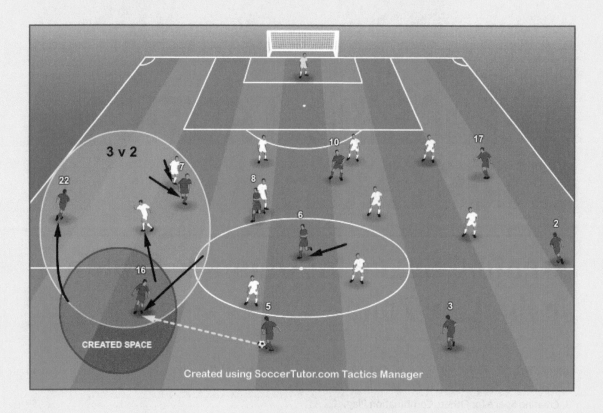

Created using SoccerTutor.com Tactics Manager

Analysis

When Barcelona were facing an opponent who used a compact formation that blocked the potential passes towards the centre of the field, and especially towards Busquets (16) and Xavi (6), the team used a tactical movement which created space in the low zone.

In this example, the full back (22) moves forward on the left flank. As the opposition's wide midfielder follows his movement, space is created in the low zone towards the left side of the pitch.

No.16 (defensive midfielder) moves to take advantage of the space in order to receive unmarked, and at the same time create superiority in numbers (3v2) on the left side.

SESSION FOR THIS TACTICAL SITUATION
(6 PRACTICES)
1. Creating Space for Others Combination Play

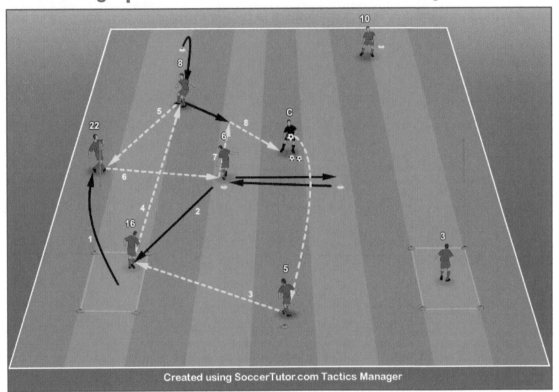

Created using SoccerTutor.com Tactics Manager

Objective
We work on creating space for others in the low zone using 3 players at the back.

Description
In this practice, we use a 40 x 40 yard area. The coach or the goalkeeper throws the ball to player 5.

As soon as No.5 receives the ball, No.22 starts moving forward. No.16 drops back to take advantage of the free space created (in the blue area). He receives from No.5 and passes towards No.8 who checks away from the cone, drops back at the right time and passes first time to No.22.

No.22 passes to No.6 who has moved towards the free space created by No.16 and No.6 passes to No.8 who then passes to the coach.

The players return quickly to their staring positions and the drill is executed towards the right side with No.6 the midfielder who drops back this time. The players use 1 or 2 touches throughout.

Coaching Points
1. The rhythm and timing of the passes to the movements is key in this exercise.
2. Players should use the correct body shape when creating a passing option so they can use 1 touch as often as possible.

VARIATION

2. Creating Space for Others Combination Play (2)

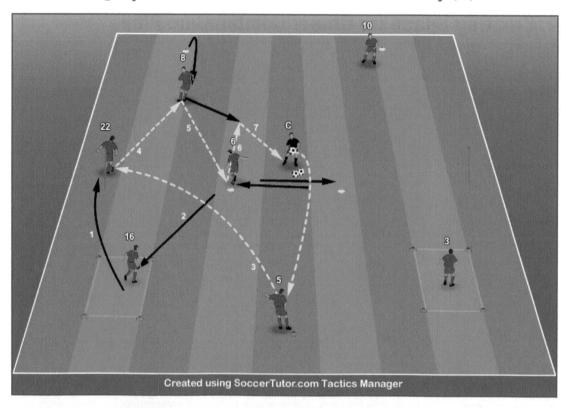

Created using SoccerTutor.com Tactics Manager

Objective

We work on creating space for others in the low zone using 3 players at the back.

Description

Here we have a variation of the previous drill. The coach or the goalkeeper throws the ball to player No.5 again to start the drill.

As soon as No.5 receives the ball, player No.22 starts moving forward. No16 drops back to take advantage of the free space created (in the blue area).

This time No.5 passes directly to player No.22 who runs round the red pole. No.8 checks away from the cone with an up and down movement to receive the pass and passes to No.6 who has moved into the free space created by No16. No.6 passes back to No.8 who passes to the coach.

The players return quickly to their staring positions and the drill is executed towards the right side with No.6 the midfielder who drops back this time. The players use 1 or 2 touches throughout.

Coaching Points

1. The rhythm and timing of the passes to the movements is key in this exercise.
2. Players should use the correct body shape when creating a passing option so they can use 1 touch as often as possible.

PROGRESSION

3. Creating Space for Others End Zone Game

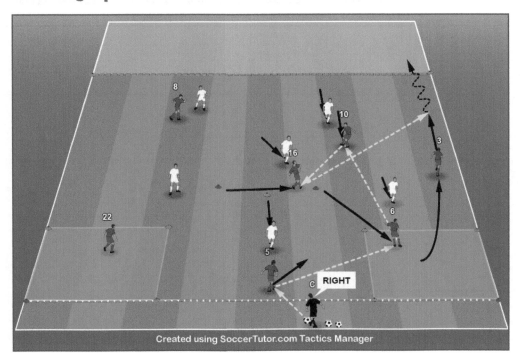

Created using SoccerTutor.com Tactics Manager

Objective

We work on creating space for others in the low zone using 3 players at the back.

Description

In an area 40 x 40 yards, we play a game with a 6v7 situation. The whites play with a 2-3-1 formation and the reds play with a 3-2-2 formation. The coach calls a side (e.g. right) and passes to the central defender who should direct the ball towards the right side.

The red team use the space inside the blue area created by the forward run of the centre back and create a numerical superiority on the right side. The reds' aim is to dribble the ball into the white zone for a player to receive the ball within this area. The whites aim to win the ball and counter attack, looking to dribble the ball through the end line.

If the ball goes out of play, the game restarts with the coach in possession and the players return to their starting positions. The 2 centre backs are inside the blue areas and the defensive midfielder is positioned on one of the blue cones (as shown). The white team's forward starts by the red cone.

If the red's are not able to achieve their aim within 10 seconds, the coach throws a ball to the white team who try to attack immediately. The offside rule is applied throughout.

Coaching Points

1. Players need to use synchronised movements to create space.

2. The team need to create available passing options as well as superiority in numbers near the sidelines.

3. Players should be aware to retain the team's balance at all times.

PROGRESSION

4. Creating Space in the Low Zone 8v7 Small Sided Game

Created using SoccerTutor.com Tactics Manager

Objective

We work on creating space for others using 3 players at the back.

Description

2 teams play an 8v7 game. The red team aims to create space in the low zone (inside the blue areas) for the defensive midfielder.

This action creates a numerical superiority on the strong side and a spare man for the red team near the sideline. The attacking team's objective is to take advantage of this situation in order to score a goal.

The white team aim to win the ball and counter attack. The blue area on the strong side must be occupied by a player during the first stage of the red team's attack. So when the centre back moves forward and out of the blue area, the defensive midfielder should drop back inside it.

As the ball moves forward near to the opposition's penalty area, the defensive midfielder can move out of the area too in order to retain the team's cohesion.

Coaching Points

1. The players need to use synchronised movements to create space (to exploit and move forward).
2. Creating available passing options, not just superiority in numbers is important.
3. Players should be aware to retain the team's balance at the back.

VARIATION

5. Creating Space in the Low Zone 9v8 Small Sided Game

Created using SoccerTutor.com Tactics Manager

Objective

We work on creating space for others using 4 players at the back.

Description

We have a variation of the previous game.

This time the red team use 4 players at the back (instead of 3) and 1 player is added to each team to create an 8v9 game.

Coaching Points

1. The players need to use synchronised movements to create space (to exploit and move forward).

2. Creating available passing options, not just superiority in numbers is important.

3. Players should be aware to retain the team's balance at the back.

PROGRESSION

6. Creating Space in the Low Zone 11v11 Game

Created using SoccerTutor.com Tactics Manager

Objective

We work on creating space for others using 3 players at the back.

Description

The 2 teams play an 11v11 game. The red team builds up using 3 defenders. The white players are not allowed in the blue areas unless the red goalkeeper makes a pass towards one of his teammates.

As soon as one of the full backs (22 or 3) moves out of a blue area, the respective defensive midfielder takes advantage of the free space inside it in order to create a numerical superiority on the strong side and maintain the defensive balance. The red team's aim is to score and the white team aim to win the ball and counter attack.

Variation

The red team plays with 4 players at the back.

Coaching Points

1. The players need to use synchronised movements to create space (to exploit and move forward).
2. Creating available passing options, not just superiority in numbers is important.
3. Players should be aware to retain the team's balance at the back.

ATTACKING TACTICAL SITUATION 6

Creating Space for Others on the Flank

ANALYSIS

CREATING SPACE FOR OTHERS ON THE FLANK

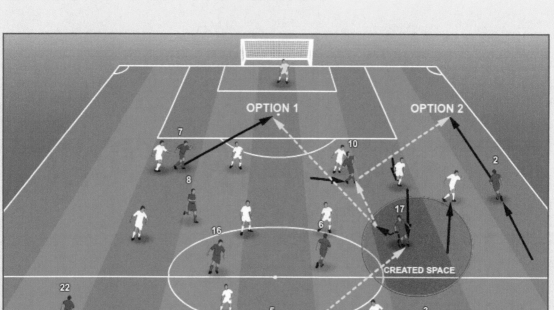

Analysis

In order for Barcelona to create space for the wingers there had to be good collaboration and synchronisation between the full backs and the wingers.

The forward movements of the full backs usually forced the opposition's wingers to follow their runs/movements. Space was created for the wingers to drop back and receive without being marked.

In this example, the full back (2) moves forward and his marker follows him. The winger (17) drops back into the space created and he has time to turn towards the opposition goal and make a pass.

The winger is then able to pass either to No.10 (Messi) or make a diagonal pass for No.7 in behind the opposition's defensive line to create a chance on goal.

SESSION FOR THIS TACTICAL SITUATION
(4 PRACTICES)
1. Creating Space for the Wingers on the Flanks Pattern of Play

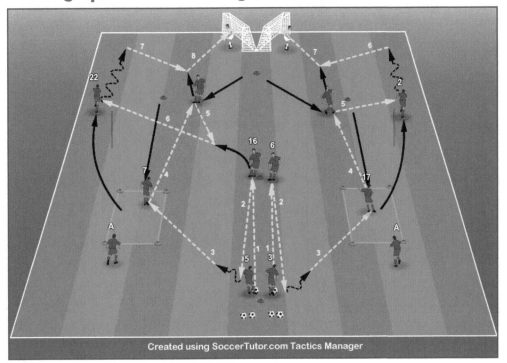

Created using SoccerTutor.com Tactics Manager

Objective

We work on creating space for the wingers on the flank using the full backs (4 players at the back).

Description

In this practice we run 2 identical passing combinations on each side which end with a shot on goal with the aim of creating space for the wingers.

Player No,5 and No.3 start by passing forward and receiving the pass back. The pass to them is the signal for the full backs to move forward round the red pole. As soon as these players start their forward movement, the wingers drop back to take advantage of the space created. They receive and pass to the forwards who have moved towards the passing lane.

After a sequence of passes, the ball ends up in the full backs' possession who hit low crosses for the centre forwards to shoot at goal. The full backs take up the role of the wingers, the wingers move out of play and the players outside (A) take up the full back roles inside the blue areas. The defensive midfielders switch positions and so do the forwards.

Coaching Points

1. The rhythm and timing of the runs with the pass is key to good attacking combinations.
2. The players need to use the correct body shape and timing so they can use just 1 touch when possible (speed up play).

PROGRESSION

2. Creating Space for the Wingers in a Dynamic 2 Zone SSG

Created using SoccerTutor.com Tactics Manager

Objective

We work on creating space for the wingers on the flank using the full backs (4 players at the back).

Description

2 teams play an 8v6 game with 2 zones and 2 mini goals. The white team uses a 2-3-1 formation and the red team uses a 4-1-3 formation. The reds aim to move the ball to the high zone and score in one of the 2 mini goals. When the full back decides to enter the high zone, the winger of the red team should drop back to the low zone in a synchronised movement.

When the white team's winger follows the full back's movement, space will be created inside the low zone. If the winger does not follow the full back's movement, a numerical advantage will be created inside the high zone.

Only the red full backs and the white wingers can move from area to area. The red wingers can enter the low zone and then move back into the high zone to create a 4v3 situation. If the white team wins the ball, there are no longer any restrictions in regards to the zones. If the ball goes out of play, the game restarts with the coach passing to a player on the red team again.

Coaching Points

1. The synchronised movement of the full back forwards and the winger dropping back is the focus of this exercise.

2. The timing of the winger's run should be at the right moment (free in space and able to turn).

3. The players should be aware to retain balance at the back at all times.

PROGRESSION

3. Creating Space on the Flank in a High & Low Zone Game

Created using SoccerTutor.com Tactics Manager

Objective

We work on creating space for the wingers on the flank using the full backs (4 players at the back).

Description

The 2 teams play a 9v9 game. The white team uses a 4-3-1 formation and the red team uses a 4-1-3 formation.

The red team aims to create space in the low zone for the wingers to drop back and receive the ball unmarked. So, when a full back enters the high zone, the respective winger drops back in a synchronised movement.

While the whites are in the defensive phase, only the wingers can move from area to area (if they want to).

If the white team win the ball, there are no limitations. The red players can move freely from area to area in any phase but they should always try to retain the team's balance.

Coaching Points

1. Correct body shape (open up on the half turn) and positioning is important to view where the next pass goes in the centre square.

2. The synchronised movement of the full back forwards and the winger dropping back is the key to creating space high up on the flank in this exercise.

3. The players should be aware to retain balance at the back at all times.

PROGRESSION

4. Wingers Dropping Deep: Creating Space 2 Zone Game

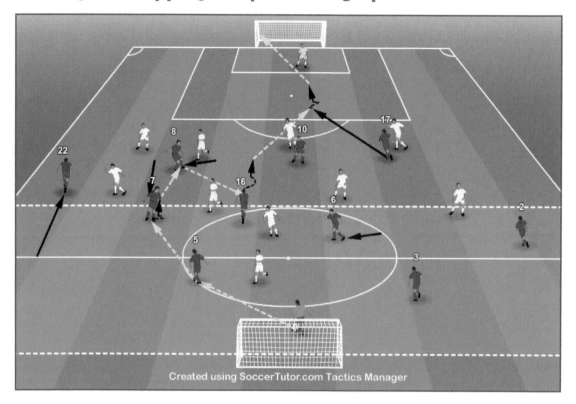

Created using SoccerTutor.com Tactics Manager

Objective

We work on creating space with the wingers dropping deep (4 players at the back).

Description

The 2 teams play a 2 zone 11v11 game. The red team build up play using 4 defenders at the back.

The red wingers and full backs work together and aim to take advantage of the free space created by the forward runs of the full backs inside the high zone. They are also aware to always retain the team's balance at the back.

The white team's defenders are not allowed to enter the low zone. The rest of the white players and all of the red players can move freely across both area.

If the white team win the ball, the restrictions are removed in regards to moving in between zones.

Coaching Points

1. Correct body shape (open up on the half turn) and positioning is important to view where the next pass goes in the centre square..

2. The judgement of the players (when to drop back, when to move forward with or without the ball) is extremely important for success in this exercise.

3. The players should be aware to retain balance at the back at all times.

ATTACKING TACTICAL SITUATION 7

Using the Correct Body Shape

ANALYSIS

USING THE CORRECT BODY SHAPE

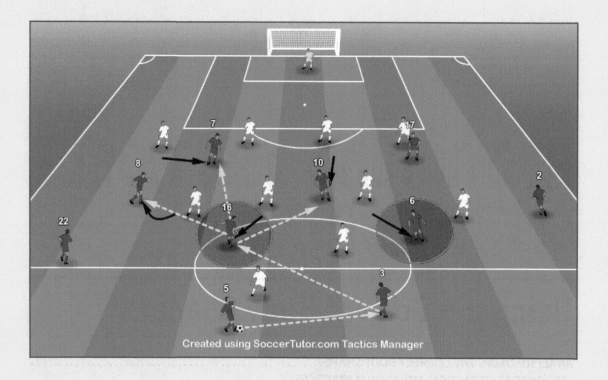

Created using SoccerTutor.com Tactics Manager

Analysis

Using the correct body shape was a basic element for Barcelona's players in order to increase their passing accuracy as well as the tempo of the team's ball circulation.

In this example, No.5 passes to No.3. As soon as the ball reaches No.3, No.16 and No.6 take up the appropriate positions using the correct body shape. This means that they are able to scan the opposition players' positions as well as their teammates' positions even before they receive the ball.

The players are able to decide in the minimum amount of time which is the best passing option. By this way they can avoid being blocked/stopped due to a possible hesitation.

Finally, in this example shown, No.16 receives and he already knows that he has 3 available passing options (8 7 & 10).

SESSION FOR THIS TACTICAL SITUATION
(4 PRACTICES)
1. Technical: Receiving with the Correct Body Shape in Pairs

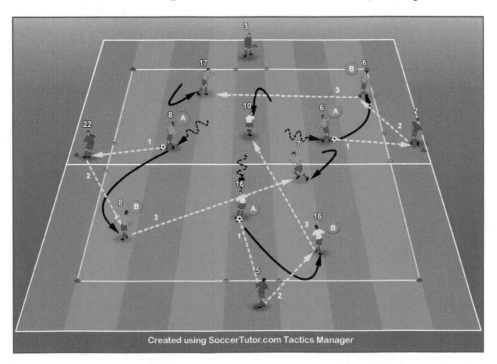

Created using SoccerTutor.com Tactics Manager

Objective

We coach the players to use the correct body shape when receiving the ball.

Description

In an area 30 x 30 yards, the players work in pairs according to their bib colour. One of them (e.g No.16) has the ball and passes towards one of the neutral players (No.5). He passes to him (position A) through the 2 small cones and then moves to the side to take up the correct body shape (position B) in order to have eye contact with his teammate (No.10) before receiving again.

The neutral player passes again to No.16 who passes to No.10 who has moved into an available passing lane (synchronised movement). The new man in possession is the one who continues the drill towards a different neutral player.

The neutral players use 2 touches to allow more time for the the receivers to move to the side and take up the correct body shape.

Coaching Points

1. Players need to take up the proper stance when receiving (open body shape).
2. Having eye contact with the teammate before receiving is very important.
3. There needs to be high quality in their passing, together with synchronised movements.

PROGRESSION

2. Using the Correct Body Shape in a 4v4 (+5) Possession Game

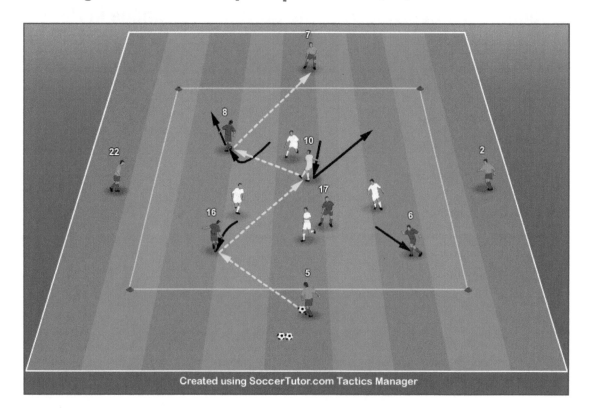

Created using SoccerTutor.com Tactics Manager

Objective

We coach the players to use the correct body shape when receiving the ball.

Description

We have an area 30 x 30 yards, with a 4v4 (+1 neutral) inside and 4 neutral players outside. The team with the ball aim to maintain possession with the help of the 5 neutrals. The aim is to to complete 10-20 passes in order to score a point.

When a player passes to an outside neutral, they move and take up the correct body shape as it helps them to be aware of the available passing options in depth before they receive again. Only the passes between the players inside the playing area count towards the completed passes needed to win a point.

The yellow player can only use 1 touch, the players inside use 2 touches and the outside players should pass the ball back into play within 3 seconds after receiving so the inside players have time to take up the correct body shape.

Coaching Points

1. The inside players should be constantly moving.
2. The correct body shape and angles should be monitored while creating passing options.
3. Having eye contact with the teammate before receiving is very important.

PROGRESSION

3. 'Receiving Zone' 6v7 (+2) Body Shape Dynamic Game

Created using SoccerTutor.com Tactics Manager

Objective

We coach the players to use the correct body shape when receiving the ball.

Description

This is an 8v6 game with 3 zones in a 40 x 50 yard area. The red team aims to score while the white team tries to win the ball and dribble the ball through the end red line.

Inside the largest zone there are 3 white defenders and 1 goalkeeper, inside the middle zone there are 2 red forwards and inside the blue low zone, there is a 4v3 situation. The red players in this zone play with 2 touches and aim to receive from the outside players using the correct body shape, being aware of the positions of the 2 red forwards. Their aim is to receive and pass the ball to 1 of the 2 forwards who move towards the available passing lanes.

All the players should stay in their own areas during the first stage of the game. However, as soon as the ball is passed to one of the forwards there is no restriction in regards to the zones. If the whites win the ball, there are also no restrictions. In these situations the players can move freely.

The outside players should only pass towards the players inside the blue area and not directly to the forwards. They should also pass within 3 seconds of receiving the ball and are allowed to pass between each other (with 1 touch only). The red forwards use 1 touch during the first stage and then they can play without restrictions.

Coaching Points

1. The inside players should be constantly moving.
2. The correct body shape and angles should be monitored while creating passing options.
3. Having eye contact with the teammate before receiving is very important.

PROGRESSION

4. 'Receiving Zone' Building Up Play 11v11 Game

Created using SoccerTutor.com Tactics Manager

Objective

We coach the players to use the correct body shape when receiving the ball.

Description

We have a 3 zone game as the teams play 2v1 in the low zone, 4v3 inside the middle blue zone and 4v6 inside the high zone. The red team aim to score after passing to a player in the middle zone who will direct it towards the forwards in the high zone. As soon as there is a pass towards the forwards, the game moves into the second phase and all the players can move freely from zone to zone.

The red players inside the low zone play without restrictions, while the red players inside the blue middle zone use 2 touches (receive and pass).

The red forwards inside the high zone only use 1 touch during the first stage (when receiving from the midfielders). During the second phase, all players play freely. If the white team win the ball they aim to counter attack and score (without any restrictions on movements between zones).

Players cannot pass directly from the low zone to the high zone.

Coaching Points

1. The players passing from the middle zone need to have the correct body shape in order to have eye contact with the forwards inside the high zone and be able to pass the ball to them as quickly as possible.

2. There should be a focus on quality passing and using the correct angles to create passing options.

ATTACKING TACTICAL SITUATION 8

Creating a Numerical Superiority on the Flanks

CREATING A NUMERICAL SUPERIORITY ON THE FLANKS

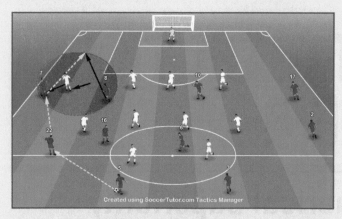

Situation 1

In this example, the attacking midfielder (8) moves diagonally behind the opposition's full back to receive in behind the defensive line.

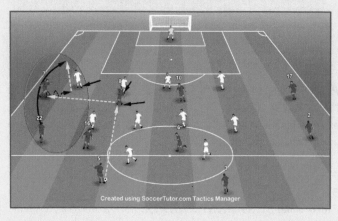

Situation 2

The overlapping run by No.22 creates a numerical advantage for Barcelona on the left flank.

Analysis

The creation of a numerical advantage/superiority on the flanks was successful for Barcelona mostly through 2 ways:

1. A diagonal movement towards the sideline and behind the opposition's full back.
2. An overlapping run by the full back.

SESSION FOR THIS TACTICAL SITUATION
(7 PRACTICES)
1. Creating a Numerical Superiority on the Flank Combination Play

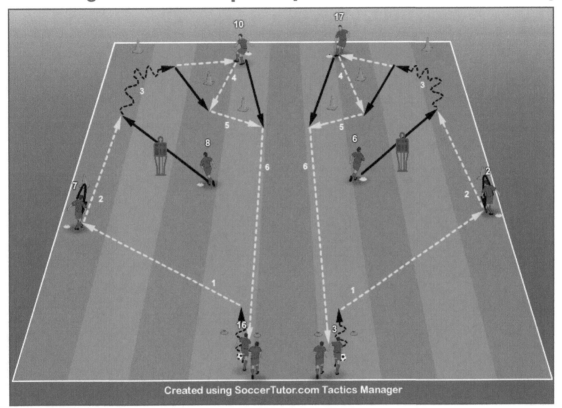

Created using SoccerTutor.com Tactics Manager

Objective

We coach the combinations/movements used to create a numerical superiority on the flank.

Description

We use an area 40 x 40 yards for this combination practice run from 2 sides. To describe the combination sequence we will use the left side as the example.

The first player (16) moves forward with the ball. As soon as he runs through the red cones, he passes diagonally to No.7 who gets free of marking after touching the cone with an up and down movement.

The new ball carrier receives and passes into the path of the diagonal movement of the attacking midfielder (8) behind the mannequin. He receives, moves with speed towards the red traffic cone and quickly changes direction (as shown in the diagram).

Finally, he plays a double 1-2 combination with No.10, who then passes with accuracy through the 2 red cones to the starting point for the next player waiting. No. 16 moves into No.7's place, 7 to 8, 8 to 10 and No.10 moves to the start.

VARIATION

2. Creating a Numerical Superiority on the Flank Combination Play (2)

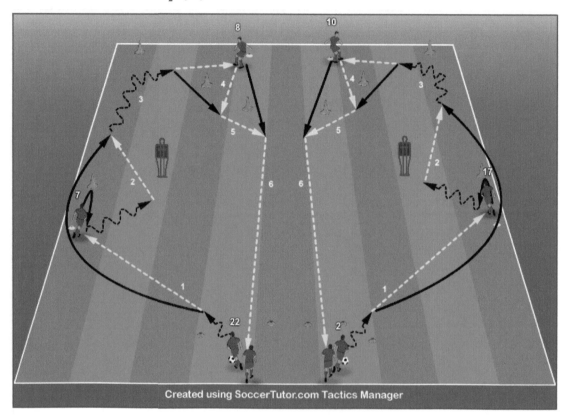

Created using SoccerTutor.com Tactics Manager

Objective

We coach the combinations/movements used to create a numerical superiority on the flank.

Description

Here we have a variation of the previous drill, with it being run from 2 sides again (as shown). To describe the combination sequence we will use the left side as the example.

No.22 moves forward with the ball. As soon as he runs through the red cones he passes diagonally to No.7 who gets free of marking after touching the red cone with an up and down movement.

The new ball carrier receives and moves towards the inside. No.22 makes an overlapping run, receives, moves with speed towards the red traffic cone and quickly changes direction.

Finally, No.22 plays a double 1-2 with No.8, before No.8 then directs the ball with accuracy through the 2 red cones to the starting point. No.22 moves to No.8's position and No.8 moves to the start. No.7 stays in the same position.

Coaching Point

The focus here is on quality passing, synchronised movements and attacking the free space.

PROGRESSION

3. Attacking Combination Play on the Flank

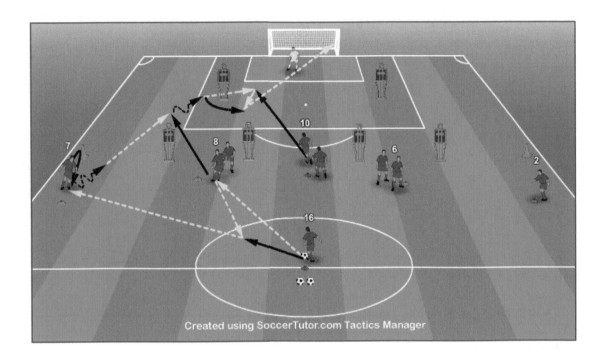

Created using SoccerTutor.com Tactics Manager

Objective

We coach the players to create and take advantage of a numerical superiority on the flank.

Description

In this exercise we practice passing combinations using half a full size pitch.

No.16 passes to No.8 and receives the pass back. He then passes to the winger (7) who checks away from the cone before receiving.

At the same time, the attacking midfielder (8) makes a diagonal run to receive in the free space behind the mannequin (opposition's right full back).

No.8 dribbles the ball inside, plays a short pass to the striker who has run into the box and gets the return pass (back heel) in order to shoot in the goal. Run the drill from both sides.

Coaching Points

1. Players should attack the available space (created by synchronised movements).
2. Make sure the players use 1 touch whenever possible to speed up play, as the aim here is to achieve quick combination play.
3. Stress the importance of quality finishing so that as many moves as possible end up with a goal.

VARIATION

4. Attacking Combination Play on the Flank (2)

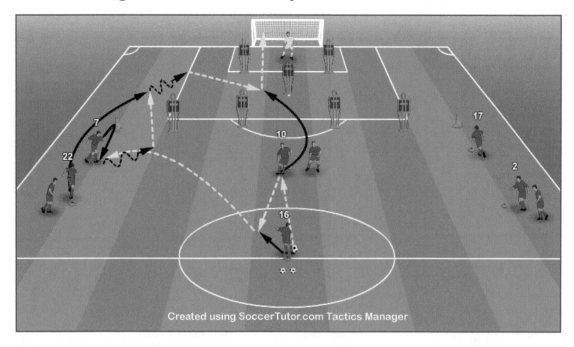

Created using SoccerTutor.com Tactics Manager

Objective

We coach the players to create and take advantage of a numerical superiority on the flank.

Description

We use half a full pitch again with 7 mannequins and a goalkeeper as shown.

No.16 plays the first pass to No10, receives the pass back and plays a long ball towards the winger who checks away from the cone (to replicate getting free from a marker).

No.7 dribbles inside and passes towards the full back who has already made the overlapping run.

The full back crosses low towards the striker who makes a movement through the mannequins to receive and finish. Run the drill from both sides.

Coaching Points

1. Stress the importance of accurate crossing and quality finishing.
2. Players should always receive the ball on the move, making sure to use the correct body shape.
3. Make sure the players use 1 touch whenever possible to speed up play, as the aim here is to achieve quick combination play.

VARIATION

5. Attacking Combination Play on the Flank (3)

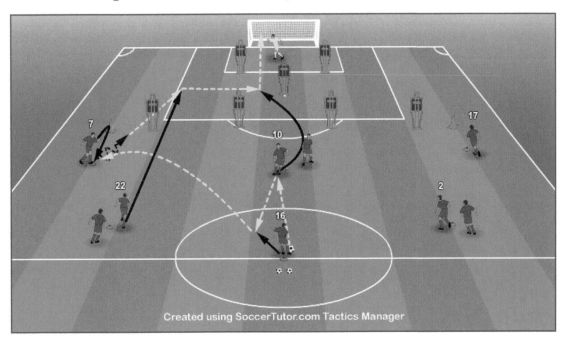

Created using SoccerTutor.com Tactics Manager

Objective

We coach the players to create and take advantage of a numerical superiority on the flank.

Description

Here we have a variation of the previous drill. No.16 passes to No10, receives back and plays a long ball towards the winger who checks away from the cone to get free of marking.

The winger (7) dribbles inside and passes towards the full back who has already made the inside run behind the mannequin's back.

The full back crosses low towards the striker who makes a run through the mannequins to receive and finish. Run the drill from both sides.

PROGRESSION

6. Switching Play to the Weak Side 9v8 Small Sided Game

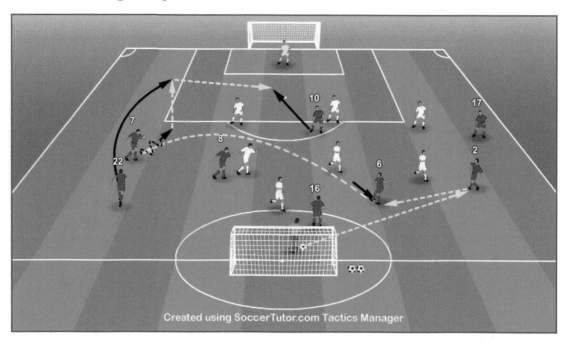

Created using SoccerTutor.com Tactics Manager

Objective

We coach the players to create and take advantage of a numerical superiority on the flank. We also work on switching play towards the weak side of the opposition.

Description

2 teams play a 9v8 game. The red team's formation is 3-2-3 and the white team's formation is 3-3-1.

The reds start and aim to score. If the white team win the ball they counter attack and try to score.

As the white team only have 3 defenders it is difficult for them to cover the entire width of the field.

This means that the red team can easily create a numerical advantage on the flanks by switching play quickly and using overlapping runs by the full backs or diagonal inside runs in behind the opposition full backs by the attacking midfielders.

Coaching Points

1. The emphasis of this practice should be to switch play frequently towards the weak side of the opposition.
2. Players should be constantly moving, while using synchronised movements and attacking the available space.

PROGRESSION

7. Creating 2v1 Situations on the Flank in a Side Zone SSG

Created using SoccerTutor.com Tactics Manager

Objective

We coach the players to create and take advantage of a numerical superiority on the flank.

Description

2 teams play an 11v11 game using 2/3 of a full pitch. There are 2 yellow zones (15 X 40 yards) on the flanks (as shown in the diagram). Only the white team's full backs are allowed in these zones, which enables the red team to create a numerical superiority near the sidelines.

Creating a numerical advantage can be achieved by the use of diagonal runs behind the full back or with overlapping runs and inside runs from the full backs. The red team aim to take advantage of there only being 1 white player allowed in each side zone, in order to create 2v1 situations on the flanks, get in behind and score.

If the white team win the ball, there are no restrictions and they can move freely across zones.

Coaching Points

1. The emphasis of this practice should be to switch play frequently towards the weak side of the opposition.
2. Players should be constantly moving, while using synchronised movements and attacking the available space.

ATTACKING TACTICAL SITUATION 9

Creating at Least 3 Passing Options for the Man in Possession

ANALYSIS

CREATING AT LEAST 3 PASSING OPTIONS FOR THE MAN IN POSSESSION

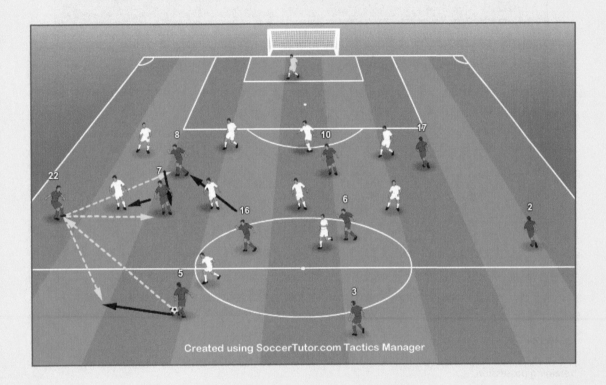

Created using SoccerTutor.com Tactics Manager

Analysis

Retaining possession easily during the attacking phase was one of Barcelona's main strengths and characteristics.

In order for Barcelona to reach their high percentages of ball possession, the players needed high technical quality, constant mobility as well as creating many passing options for the player in possession.

This was especially true in situations when the ball was near the sidelines, where it was easier for the opposition to block Barca. The players would look to create at least 3 passing options.

In this example, there is a pass towards the full back (22). Creating a numerical advantage on the flank is not easy in this situation and the team are not able to move into the third stage of attack.

The players around the ball zone move towards the potential passing lanes to provide at least 3 passing options. With these passing options, Barca are able to move the ball to another part of the pitch which will better favour moving into the third stage of attack.

SESSION FOR THIS TACTICAL SITUATION
(4 PRACTICES)
1. Switching Play '4 Corner Zones' Possession Game

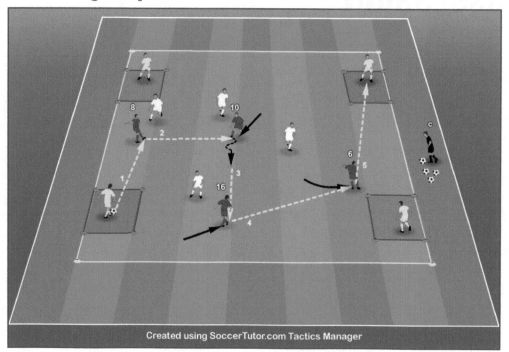

Created using SoccerTutor.com Tactics Manager

Objective

We work on switching play diagonally by providing at least 3 passing options for the neutral players and retaining possession.

Description

In an area 30 x 30 yards, 2 teams play a 4v4 game. There are also 4 neutral players, 1 in a square zone in each corner who play with the team in possession. The 2 teams inside the area aim to retain possession and switch the play from 1 neutral player to the neutral player in the opposite corner (1 point). However, the players inside have to make at least 2 passes before they can pass to the neutral player in the opposite corner.

The players in possession try to form the correct shapes (rhombus & triangles) in order to provide as many passing options as possible (3 passing options is ideal) to make the retention of possession easier. They can pass the ball to any neutral player to maintain possession. However, points are only scored when the diagonal switch of play is achieved.

The neutral players should pass within 3 seconds of receiving. If they do not, the coach passes a new ball to the opposition and the game continues with them in possession.

Coaching Points

1. The correct body shape should be monitored (opening up) and receiving/passing with the back foot (foot furthest away from the ball).

2. There should be constant mobility towards the potential passing lanes/options.

PROGRESSION

2. Creating Passing Options in a Dynamic End Line Game

Created using SoccerTutor.com Tactics Manager

Objective

We work on switching play by providing at least 3 passing options for the neutral players and retaining possession.

Description

In an area 30 x 40 yards, 2 teams play a 6v6 game with 2 neutral players outside. The aim is to move the ball from 1 neutral to the other after completing at least 2 passes between the inside players and then try to dribble the ball through the end line.

The players in possession can pass the ball back to the neutral player from whom they received in order to avoid losing possession.

The neutral players should pass within 3 seconds of receiving. If they do not, the coach passes a new ball to the opposition and the game continues with them in possession.

Coaching Points

1. The players should be constantly aware to take up the correct positions to facilitate the switching of play.
2. The correct body shape should be monitored, allowing the players to use 1 touch (speed up play).

PROGRESSION

3. Switching Play 7v7 (+2) Small Sided Game

Created using SoccerTutor.com Tactics Manager

Objective

We work on switching play by providing at least 3 passing options for the neutral players and retaining possession.

Description

This is a progression of the previous small sided game in an area 35 x 45 yards. The 2 teams play 6v6 with 2 outside neutral players.

The teams aim to move the ball from 1 neutral to the other while completing at least 2 passes between themselves and then they try to score.

The players in possession can pass the ball back to the neutrals who they received from in order to maintain possession.

The neutral players should pass within 3 seconds of receiving. If they do not, the coach passes a new ball to the opposition and the game continues with them in possession.

PROGRESSION

4. Switching Play to the Flank in a 9v9 (+2) Side Zone Game

Created using SoccerTutor.com Tactics Manager

Objective

We work on switching play by providing at least 3 passing options for the neutral players and retaining possession.

Description

2 teams play an 8v8 game with 2 neutrals inside the zones on the sidelines. The teams seek to move the ball from 1 neutral to the other after completing at least 2 passes between themselves and then they try to score.

The players in possession can pass the ball back to the neutral player who they received from in order to avoid losing possession.

The neutral players can use 2 touches or pass within 3 seconds of receiving.

ATTACKING TACTICAL SITUATION 10

Receiving in Behind the Midfield Line and Approaching the Third Stage of Attack

ANALYSIS

RECEIVING IN BEHIND THE MIDFIELD LINE AND APPROACHING THE THIRD STAGE OF ATTACK

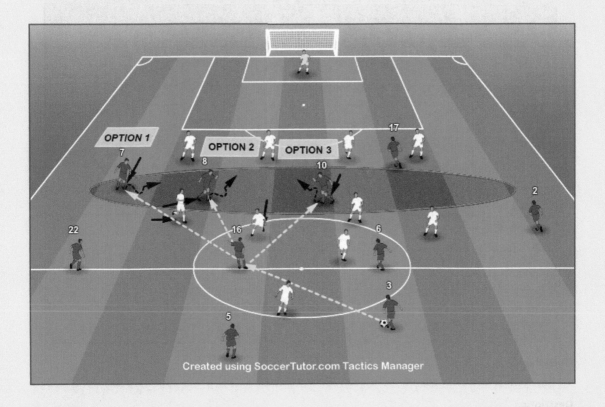

Analysis

Barcelona could approach the third stage of attack when the forwards or the midfielders had the opportunity to receive in the space behind the opposition's midfielders unmarked.

When this situation occurred, Barcelona's players could turn towards the opposition's goal and play a final pass (in behind the defensive line).

In this example. No.16 receives the ball in the middle of the pitch with the correct body shape (facing the opposition goal) and has 3 passing options which can all then lead to the third stage of attack and with a final pass.

SESSION FOR THIS TACTICAL SITUATION
(6 PRACTICES)
1. Receive, Turn and Pass in Limited Space

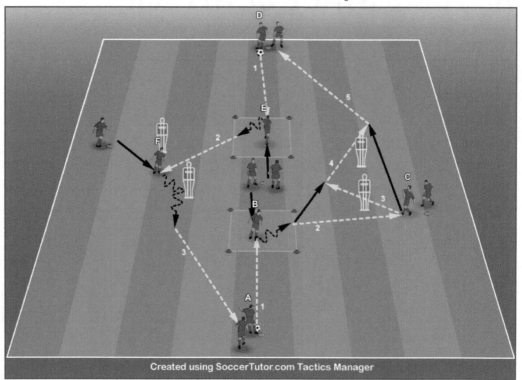

Created using SoccerTutor.com Tactics Manager

Objective

We train the players to turn and pass with limited space and time.

Description

In an area 40 x 40 yards we run a drill with 2 balls, working on turning within a limited space, using 2 different passing patterns.

Player A passes to B as soon as he has made a movement towards the blue area. B turns within the blue area and passes to C. Player C and B play a double 1-2 and the ball ends up at the other end.

At the same time on the other side, Player D passes to E who turns within the blue area and passes to F who makes a well timed run behind the first mannequin. Player F receives and dribbles the ball towards the second mannequin and performs a feint/change of direction. He then passes to the other side.

The first and last passes should be as close to being at the same time as possible. The size of the blue area will depend on the level of the players.

Coaching Points

1. When the players are turning, they should use soft touches to keep the ball close to their feet.
2. Passes should be accurate and well timed with the movements/runs of the player receiving.

PROGRESSION

2. Receive, Turn, Pass and Switch Play Possession Game

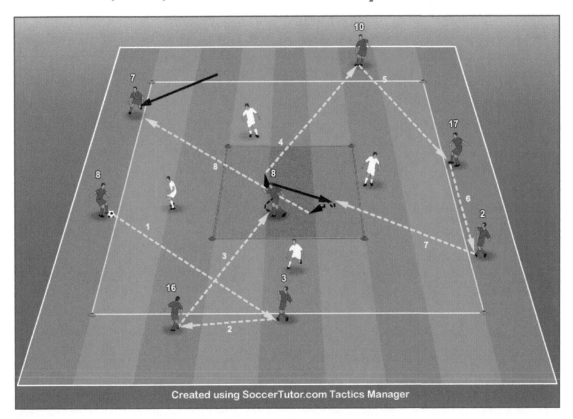

Created using SoccerTutor.com Tactics Manager

Objective

We train the players to turn and pass in limited space and time with switching play.

Description

In an area 30 x 30 yards, there is an 8v4 situation. 7 red players take up positions outside of the playing area and 1 red player is positioned inside a smaller centre square. The red players (in possession) aim to retain the ball and find a way to pass the ball to the player inside the red area.

The player inside has to turn and pass using only 2 touches.

The outside players can move from side to side in order to find an available passing lane to pass the ball to the player inside. The red players score a point if they complete 15 consecutive passes or if they manage to pass twice to the player inside and he switches play successfully.

The white players are not allowed to enter the red area at any time. They switch positions with 4 of the red players every 2 minutes.

Coaching Points

1. The players should be constantly moving towards the available passing options.

2. Emphasis the importance of quality in passing and turning.

PROGRESSION

3. Receive, Turn and Pass 3 Zone Switching Play Game

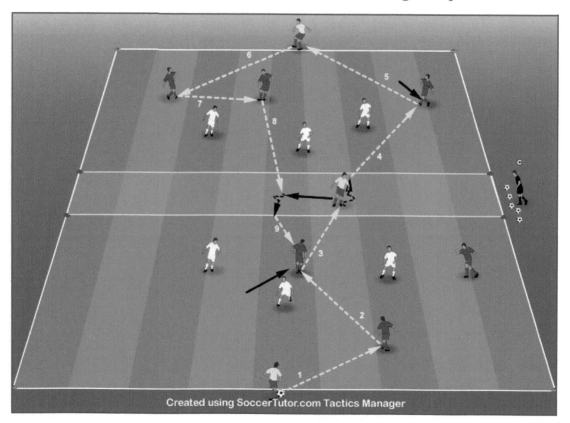

Created using SoccerTutor.com Tactics Manager

Objective

We work on switching play by turning, passing and retaining possession.

Description

We play a 3 zone game in an area 30 x 30 yards (with a 7 x 30 yard central zone). There is a 3v3 situation inside the 2 end zones, 1 neutral player inside the central zone and 2 neutral players outside of the playing area (at the ends).

The red's aim to retain possession and find a way to pass the ball to the neutral player inside the central zone. This player should then turn and pass to a red player on the other side. The red players on the other side have to pass the ball to the neutral outside before passing back to the neutral inside.

A player can pass the ball more than once to the neutral outside in order to retain possession. The roles switch in 2 ways; the team in possession only have 20 seconds to pass the ball to the neutral inside or the coach plays a ball in to the other team or if the defending team win the ball, they carry on with the roles switched.

The outside neutral players use 1 touch or pass within 3 seconds of receiving. The neutral player inside the central zone use 2 touches, as do the team in possession.

PROGRESSION

4. Passing Through the Midfield Line Possession Game

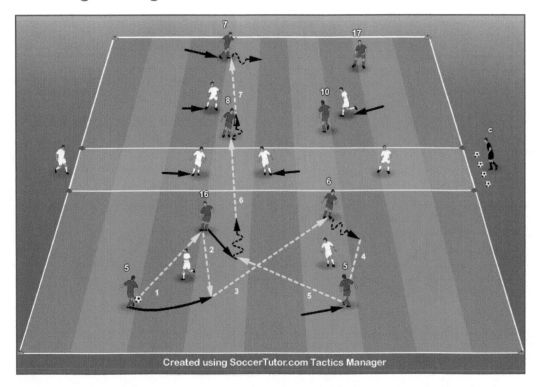

Created using SoccerTutor.com Tactics Manager

Objective

We work on passing the ball in behind the opposition's midfield line (and receiving).

Description

We use the same area as the previous drill and play 4v2 in both end zones. There are also 3 white players inside the central zone (+1 outside at the side).

The red players inside the low zone aim to retain possession and pass the ball towards the red players at the opposite end, evading the 3 white players in the middle. The red players inside the high zone should receive, retain possession and then try to pass back to the low zone.

If the white team intercept/win the ball, they play 5v4 as the 3 players in the middle move into an end zone with the aim of completing 10 passes. If they lose possession, they go back to their starting positions.

There can be a restriction for the reds e.g. to complete 4 passes or achieve the switch of play within 20 seconds. If they are unable to do this, the coach blows their whistle and passes a new ball to the white players to play 6v4.

Variation

When the whites win possession, they play 5v4 inside one white area and the coach passes a new ball into the opposite area where the teams play 4v3 in favour of the reds (the outside white player enters this area). The teams compete and maintain possession as long as possible. If the whites win, they switch positions with the reds and the game restarts with them in possession.

PROGRESSION

5. Passing Through the Midfield Line Dynamic SSG

Created using SoccerTutor.com Tactics Manager

Objective

We work on turning, passing and approaching the third stage of attack.

Description

The 2 teams play 6v6 (+GK) in the low zone with 3 extra red players positioned behind the receiving red zone.

The 6 red players seek to retain possession and then find a way to pass the ball to one of the 3 forwards who drop back at the right time inside the red area to receive on the turn and try to score in 1 of the 2 small goals.

The white team defends and tries to win/intercept the ball, counter attack and score. The red team uses a maximum of 2 touches and the white team plays without restrictions.

Coaching Points

1. The players need to drop back at the right time to create superiority in numbers.
2. The players should be constantly moving and creating angles for the passing lane.

PROGRESSION

6. Passing Through the Midfield Line 'Receiving Zone' Game

Created using SoccerTutor.com Tactics Manager

Objective

We work on turning, passing and approaching the third stage of attack.

Description

Using 2/3 of a full pitch with 2 zones 10 yards in length, we play 11v11. There is a 6v4 situation in favour of the reds in the low zone and a 4v4 situation in the high zone.

The red players inside the high zone can drop back inside the red zone and receive without marking (the white players are not allowed in this zone). The red team's aim is to move the ball to the players who drops back inside the red zone and then try to score.

The red player who receives the pass inside the red area must use 2 touches and pass within the area. He can pass in behind the opposition's defence (or in front of it if there is no potential passing lane for a through ball).

The 2 white defensive midfielders are positioned inside the white zone and try to intercept the through passes. However, as soon as the ball has moved into the high zone or the whites win the ball at any time, everyone can then move freely across all zones. The white team aim to win the ball and score (counter attack).

ATTACKING TACTICAL SITUATION 11

Breaking Through the Opposition's Pressing in the First Stage of Attack Using 2 Players at the Back

ANALYSIS

BREAKING THROUGH THE OPPOSITION'S PRESSING IN THE FIRST STAGE OF ATTACK USING 2 PLAYERS AT THE BACK

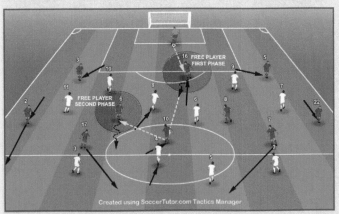

Created using SoccerTutor.com Tactics Manager

Situation 1

In the first example, the opposition played with 2 forwards. As No.16 drops back, there is a 3v2 situation and No.16 is the free player and receives the pass from the goalkeeper.

As soon as the opposition midfielder (8) moves to close No.16 down, Barca's No.6 (Xavi) becomes free of marking (second phase free player) and receives the ball via No.10.

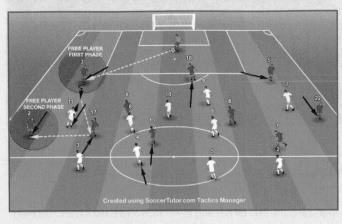

Created using SoccerTutor.com Tactics Manager

Situation 2

In the second situation, the opposition play with 3 forwards. No.16 drops back again but the white No.9 is close to him. The white No.7 takes up a balanced position to cover both No.5 and No.22. So Dani Alves (2) moves into an advanced position and forces the white No.11 to follow his movement.

No.3 becomes the first phase free player and receives the ball from the goalkeeper. As soon as he is put under pressure by No.11, No.2 becomes the second phase free player and receives via No.17.

Analysis

Barcelona would often build up play starting from the goalkeeper, mainly using short passes despite the opposition pressing high up the pitch. The team's ability to break through the opposition's pressing was based on the players' technical ability as well as their ability to read the tactical situations and recognise who was the free player quickly in order to pass him the ball.

When the team used 2 players at the back and had to deal with the opposition's pressure in the build up phase, the defensive midfielder (16) dropped back between the 2 centre backs, the centre backs would move towards the sidelines and the full backs would move into advanced positions. There was always a free player to receive a pass from the goalkeeper when the opposition played with 2 or 3 forwards. Messi's (10) positioning deeper also created superiority in numbers for Barcelona in midfield.

SESSION FOR THIS TACTICAL SITUATION
(6 PRACTICES)
1. Building Up From the Back Pattern of Play

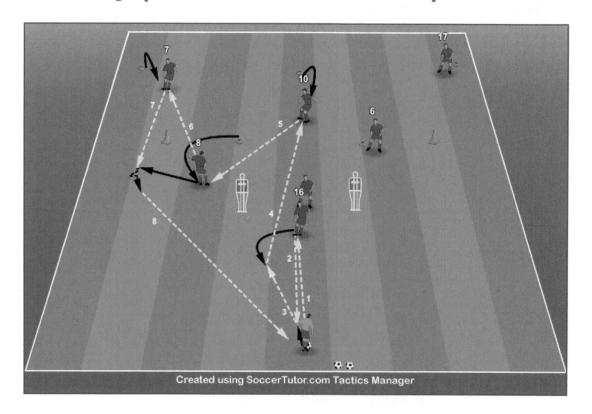

Created using SoccerTutor.com Tactics Manager

Objective

We work on breaking through the opposition's pressing in the first stage using 2 players at the back.

Description

We use an area 30 x 30 yards and the goalkeeper starts the drill by passing to No.16. No.16 passes back and then drops back to receive on the half turn (open body shape). As soon as No.16 receives, No.10 makes a movement to get free of marking and the centre midfielder on the left side (8) moves towards a passing lane with an open body shape.

No.16 passes forward to No.10 and after a sequence of passes (as shown) the ball ends up back in the goalkeeper's possession. No.8 moves into No7's position, 10 to 8 and 7 to 10. No.16 goes back to his starting position. Then the drill is executed towards the right side.

Coaching Points

1. Correct body shape (open up on the half turn) and positioning is important to view where the next pass is going.

2. Good communication, movement and vision are essential for this exercise.

PROGRESSION

2. Quick Combination Play with the 'Link Players'

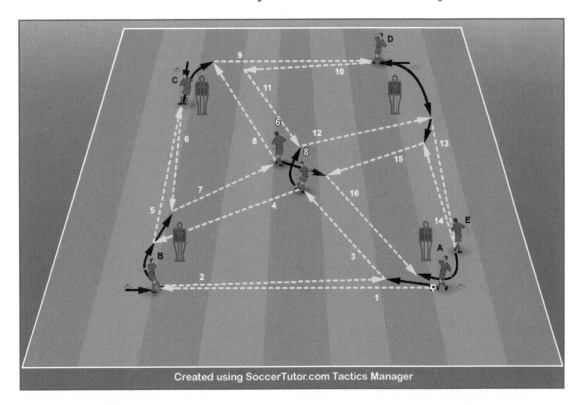

Created using SoccerTutor.com Tactics Manager

Objective
We work on the 'link player' when breaking through the opposition's pressing in the first stage using 2 players at the back.

Description
In an area 30 x 30 yards we have a passing combination with 2 link players in the centre.

Player A plays a 1-2 combination with player B. Player A passes towards one of the centre players (8) who passes in front of the mannequin for B's run round the mannequin.

After the combination of passes between B and C, the ball is passed towards the other centre player (6) who passes in front of the other mannequin for C. The sequence continues with the order of passes shown in the diagram.

Player A takes up position B, B to C, C to D, D to E and E to A. The players use 1 touch.

Coaching Points
1. The movements need to be synchronised with well timed passes out in front of the players to move onto without having to slow down.
2. The body shape of the 'link players' is key, as they open up to pass at different angles.
3. The passes of the link player should be made with the back foot (furthest away from the ball).

PROGRESSION

3. Building Up Play From the Back to Break Through Pressing

Created using SoccerTutor.com Tactics Manager

Objective

We work on breaking through the opposition's pressing in the first stage of the build up play.

Description

In an area 40 x 40 yards, the goalkeeper starts this practice by playing a long ball to the other goalkeeper. The other goalkeeper catches the ball and No.16 drops back. No.5 moves towards the sideline and No.22 moves forward in a synchronised movement.

The ball is directed to No.16 who passes to No5. As soon as No.5 receives, No.8 drops back, receives and passes to No.22. No.22 moves forward with the ball and crosses low towards No10 to finish. In the diagram, we have an example where No.10 has missed the cross, so No.8 has followed in to finish at the back post.

No.16 and No.5 switch positions, No.22 returns to his starting position and No.8 and No.10 switch positions. The drill is then executed towards the right side.

PROGRESSION

4. Finding the Target Player in a 4v4 (+4) Switching Play Game

Created using SoccerTutor.com Tactics Manager

Objective

In this practice we work on finding a specific player free of marking.

Description

In an area 30 x 30 yards, we have a 4v4 inside the area with 4 neutral players outside. 1 of the players of the team in possession carries a yellow bib.

This bib makes that player the target player (the player who should pass the ball towards the opposite side). The bib can be passed to one of his teammates even when the ball is inside the marked area (in case the opposition use man marking against the player who has it).

To start, one of the neutral players enters the marked area with the ball. This action creates a numerical advantage for the team in possession (5v4). The target player is No.17 and the red players need to pass the ball to him. As soon as he receives and passes the ball towards the opposite side, his team score a point.

If the whites win the ball, they have the same aim as they use the yellow bib. The neutral player inside the area returns to his starting position as soon as the team's aim is achieved. The team in possession can pass the ball to the outside neutral players in order to avoid losing possession. In this situation, the neutral player can only use 1 touch.

Variation

You can introduce 2 bibs for the team in possession to make it easier for the players to find the target player.

Progression

The coach sets a specific time limit (e.g. 10 seconds) for the team in possession to achieve their aim. If they are unable to do it in time, the ball is overturned to the other team.

Coaching Points

1. Correct body shape (open up on the half turn) and positioning is important to view where the next pass is going.
2. The players should be constantly moving, trying to create the right angles to provide passing options.

PROGRESSION

5. Building Up 'Free Player' Dynamic End Line Game

Created using SoccerTutor.com Tactics Manager

Objective

We work on breaking through the opposition's pressing in the first stage of the build up play.

Description

In this small sided game, there is an 8v6 situation in favour of the red team. The red players are positioned on the red cones as shown. The game starts with the coach's long ball towards the goalkeeper. As soon as the goalkeeper catches the ball, the red players move to take up their starting positions for the build up to start.

The red team aim to find a way to dribble the ball through the halfway line after passing the ball to the free player without using a long ball. The white players try to win the ball and launch a counter attack (aiming to score past the goalkeeper).

In this example shown, the defensive midfielder (16) drops into a centre back's position and the 2 centre backs move towards the sidelines. This formation makes it difficult for the opposition to deal with while they try to press, as there is always a free man available.

When the attacking move is finished, the red players move back to their starting positions on the cones. To follow, there are 4 examples of how this exercise can be executed.

Coaching Points

1. All players need to be able to read the tactical situation, so they can quickly react and make the correct movements and decisions.
2. With intelligent movement, there should always be a free player to work the ball to.

Example 1

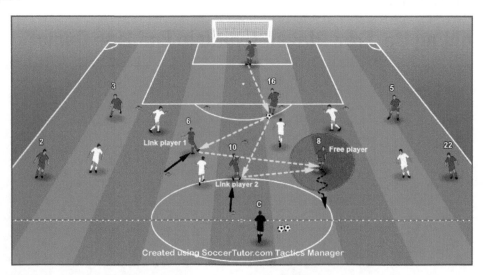

In this example, when No16 receives he is put under pressure from the opposition's midfielders. This cohesive pressure high up the pitch allows the red's No.8 to get free of marking.

As No.16 is unable to pass the ball directly to No.8, both No.6 and No.10 move into passing lanes to become link players.

Example 2

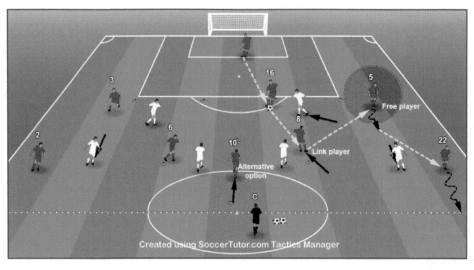

In this example, No16 is put under pressure by the opposition forward. No.5 becomes the free player and No.8 the link player to pass the ball to him.

There is then is a 2v1 situation on the flank and the red team can easily achieve the aim of dribbling the ball through the halfway line.

Example 3

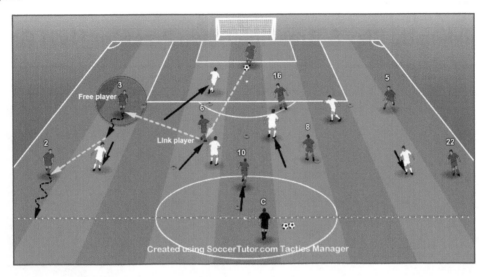

In this third example, the pressure is applied directly to the goalkeeper. No.3 becomes the free player and the ball is passed to him through the link player (6).

Example 4

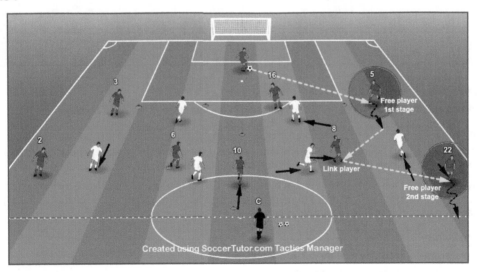

In the final example, the opposition's forwards are in positions which prevent the passes towards No.3 and No.16.

The goalkeeper passes to No.5 who is the free player and then through No.8, the ball is passed to the second phase's free player (22) to dribble over the halfway line.

PROGRESSION

6. Building Up Play & Breaking Down Pressure 11v11 Game

Created using SoccerTutor.com Tactics Manager

Objective

We work on breaking through the opposition's pressing in the first stage of the build up play.

Description

The 2 teams play an 11v11 game. The red team aims to build up play from the goalkeeper using 2 players at the back without using long passes. The white team defend try to win the ball and launch a counter attack.

The only restriction for the white players is that the 2 centre backs are not allowed to leave their zone (white) during the defensive phase. This creates a numerical advantage for the red team inside the main zone of play, as No.10 can drop back inside this area without being marked.

Coaching Points

1. The players need to quickly read the tactical situation.
2. The focus is on working the ball to find the free man.
3. Synchronised movements are used to create available passing options.
4. Correct body shape and quality passing (well timed and weighted) are very important.

ATTACKING TACTICAL SITUATION 12

Breaking Through the Opposition's Pressing in the First Stage of Attack Using 3 Players at the Back

ANALYSIS

BREAKING THROUGH THE OPPOSITION'S PRESSING IN THE FIRST STAGE OF ATTACK USING 3 PLAYERS AT THE BACK

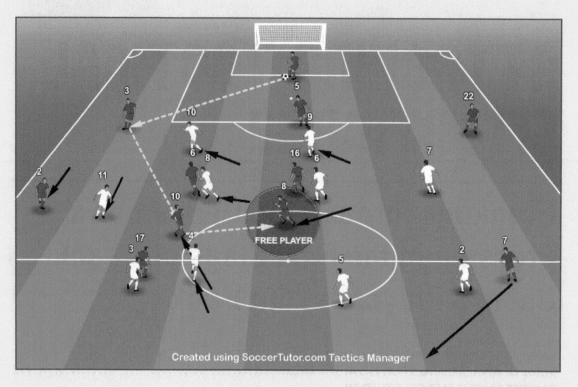

Created using SoccerTutor.com Tactics Manager

Analysis

In this tactical situation, Barcelona are using 3 players at the back as Dani Alves (2) moves into a more advanced position. The 3 man defence makes it difficult for the opposition to apply pressure high up the pitch.

In this example, the 2 opposition forwards are positioned close to Barcelona's penalty area (to be able to apply pressure to the defenders immediately). The white midfielders are in advanced positions too, in order to be close to Barca's No.6 and No.16.

Barcelona's free player here is No.8 (the target player). Messi's position deeper in the field creates superiority in numbers and he becomes the link player who passes the ball to No.8.

In order for the team to train in this tactical situation all exercises (1-4) from the previous chapter can be used as well as the variation of exercise 6 which is presented with 3 examples on the following 2 pages.

PRACTICE FOR THIS TACTICAL SITUATION

Building Up Play From the Back Dynamic End Line Game

Created using SoccerTutor.com Tactics Manager

Objective

We work on breaking through the opposition's pressing in the first stage of the build up play.

Description

This small sided game is a variation of exercise 5 in the previous tactical situation, with the red team using 3 players at the back this time. There is an 8v6 situation in favour of the red team and the players are positioned on the red cones.

The game starts with the coach's long ball towards the goalkeeper. As soon as he catches the ball, the red players move to take up their starting positions. They try to find a way to dribble the ball through the halfway line after passing the ball to the free player (without using long balls). The white players aim to win the ball and launch a counter attack.

In this example, when the goalkeeper catches the ball, the right full back moves into a midfielder's position higher up the pitch. The other 3 defenders form a trio at the back while the defensive midfielder drops a few yards back and is the free player most of the time.

In case an opponent marks him, 1 of the 2 attacking midfielders stays free of marking. No.10 will then become he link player. This formation makes it difficult for the opposition to deal with when applying pressure as there is always a free man available.

When the attacking move is finished, the red players move back to their starting positions by the cones. To follow, there are 3 more examples of how this exercise can be executed.

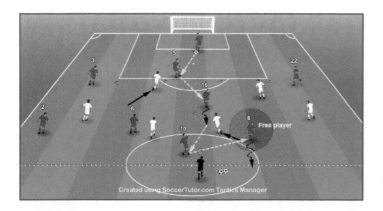

Example 1

In this example, the defensive midfielder (16) receives unmarked and moves forward with the ball. As soon as one of the opposition's centre midfielders moves to close him down, No.8 becomes free of marking.

At the same time, No.10 drops back towards an available passing lane in order to become a link player in case the direct pass towards No.8 is blocked.

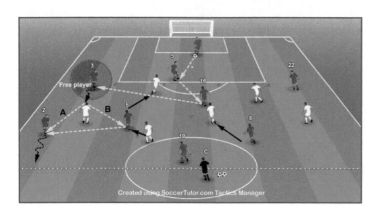

Example 2

In this example, No.5 receives the ball and is under pressure from the forward. This leaves the red No.3 free of marking and No.16 becomes the link player to pass the ball to him.

There is then a 2v1 situation in favour of the red team near the sideline which makes things easier in regards to the team's aim of dribbling the ball through the halfway line.

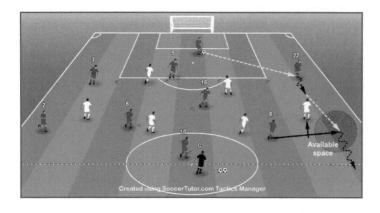

Example 3

In this example, there is a white forward who is close to the centre and blocks the potential pass to No.16.

However, No.22 is free and the goalkeeper passes to him.

No.8 makes a movement towards the sideline which creates a 2v1 situation, receives the ball and dribbles over the halfway line.

ATTACKING TACTICAL SITUATION 13

Building Up Play on the Right Flank Using a 3 Man Defence

ANALYSIS

BUILDING UP PLAY ON THE RIGHT FLANK USING A 3 MAN DEFENCE

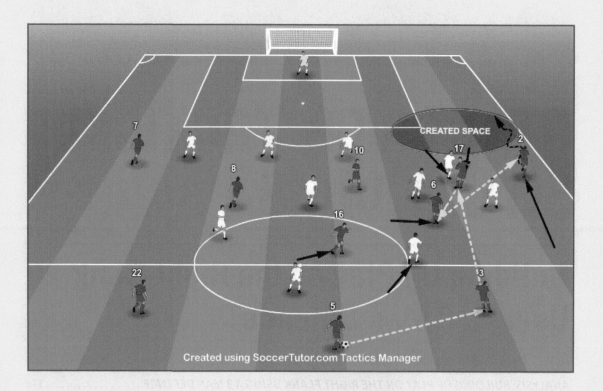

CREATED SPACE

Created using SoccerTutor.com Tactics Manager

Analysis

The use of a 3 man defence gave the right back the freedom to play in a more advanced position. Dani Alves's (2) advanced position helped the players to use several attacking combinations on the right flank.

In this example, No.2 and No.17 make coordinated movements, as the first drops back and the second moves forward. As the opposition's full back follows No.17, space is created on the flank.

Also, on this occasion, the opposition wide midfielder's positioning is poor. So after the combination between No.3, No.17 and No.6, the ball ends up in No.2's possession on the flank with plenty of space to take advantage of.

SESSION FOR THIS TACTICAL SITUATION
(5 PRACTICES)
1. Building Up on the Flank Combination Play

Created using SoccerTutor.com Tactics Manager

Objective
We practice combination play used to attack on the flank.

Description
We use an area 40 x 40 yards split into 2 sections (as shown). These passing drills are to work on the passing combinations used on the right flank.

The player at the base of the diamond (centre back) makes the first pass towards the right or left, receives the pass back and then directs the ball towards the centre. The players execute the combination shown which ends up with a shot on goal.

The players on the left move into the next position (3 to 2, 2 to 6, 6 to 17 and 17 to the other side). On the right, 3 moves to 6, 6 to 2, 2 to 17 and 17 to the other side.

Coaching Points
1. Make sure the players communicate and heads are up as they make synchronised movements.
2. Start the drill with 2 touches and quickly progress to 1 touch to speed up play.

VARIATION

2. Building Up on the Flank Combination Play (2)

Created using SoccerTutor.com Tactics Manager

Objective

We practice combination play used to attack on the flank.

Description

Here we have a variation of the previous drill. These passing drills for the players to work on passing combinations used on the right flank.

The player at the base of the diamond (centre back) makes the first pass left, receives the pass back and then directs the ball towards the other side.

The players execute the combination which ends up with a shot on goal.

The players on the left move into the next position (3 to 6, 6 to 2, 2 to 17 and 17 to the other side). On the right, 3 moves to 2, 2 to 6, 6 to 17 and 17 to the other side.

PROGRESSION

3. 4v4 (+2) Position Specific Possession Game

Created using SoccerTutor.com Tactics Manager

Objective
We use this possession game to develop attacking play on the right flank.

Description
In an area 30 x 30 yards, we play a 4v4 possession game with 2 additional outside players. The 4 red players (centre back, defensive midfielder, right back and right winger) aim to find a way to move the ball from No.5 to No.7 using at least 2 passes to win 1 point.

As soon as No.7 receives a pass, the red players move towards No.5's side to receive another ball.

The ball can be passed back to No.5 in order to maintain possession.

The white players aim to win the ball and then complete 5-7 consecutive passes (1 point).

When the ball goes out of play, No.5 passes another one in. No.5 has 10 balls which means the attacking team have 10 opportunities to attack and achieve their aim. The teams then switch roles.

No.5 is limited to 1 touch or he should pass within 3 seconds of receiving.

Progression
A maximum amount of touches can be applicable to the level of the players.

PROGRESSION

4. Attacking Combinations on the Right Flank with Finishing

Objective

We develop the attacking play on the right flank.

Description

We use a quarter of the pitch with a marked out area 30 x 30 yards. We have a 4v4 inside the area with each team having 2 extra players outside and a goalkeeper.

The 4 red players (with help from the outside players) aim to dribble the ball through the end line and shoot on goal unopposed. The red outside players are limited to 1 touch.

The white players defend and try to win the ball and pass it to one of the outside players. As soon as this takes place, there are no limitations as all players can move outside of the marked area and the teams play 6v6.

However, after winning the ball, the white team pass to their outside player and only have 8 seconds to complete their counter attack.

Progression

A restriction in the number of touches used by the red players can be applied according to the level of the players.

PROGRESSION

5. Numerical Advantage Flank Zones Game

Created using SoccerTutor.com Tactics Manager

Objective

We use this game to develop attacking play on the flanks.

Description

The 2 teams play an 11v11 game. There are 2 blue marked areas on the flanks. In these areas, there must always be a 4v3 situation in favour of the red team.

The 4 red players who enter the areas are a centre back, a full back, an attacking midfielder and a forward. The white full back, centre back and defensive midfielder can enter the marked areas too.

The red team aim to move the ball into these areas in order to take advantage of the numerical advantage. Then they seek to dribble the ball (or receive it) beyond the red line, move the ball closer to the opposition's box and score.

If the white team win the ball, there are no limitations in regards to the zones. The whites inside the blue area are not allowed to defend beyond the red line. The offside rule is applied throughout.

Progression

Limit the touches inside the blue zones applicable to the level of the players.

ATTACKING TACTICAL SITUATION 14

Switching Play

ANALYSIS
SWITCHING PLAY

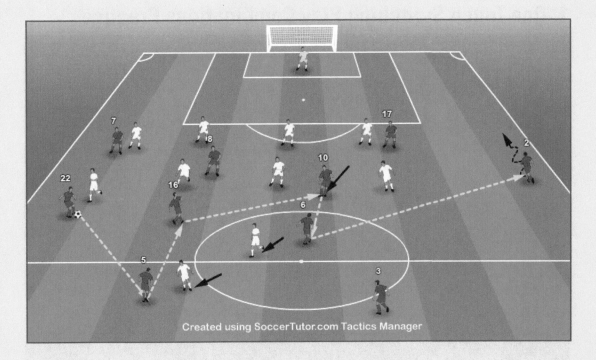

Analysis

When Barcelona could not find a way to attack down the flank (usually due to the fact that many opposition players were positioned there) they would look to move the ball to the opposition's weak side.

In this example Barcelona's players create 3 passing options for No.22, who decides to pass back to No.5 and the switch of play is achieved through a passing combination between No.16, No.10 and No.6 using mainly 1 touch play.

Constant mobility, good positioning and quality technique were the key elements to have a successful switch of play.

SESSION FOR THIS TACTICAL SITUATION
(4 PRACTICES)
1. One Touch Switching Play Combinations Practice

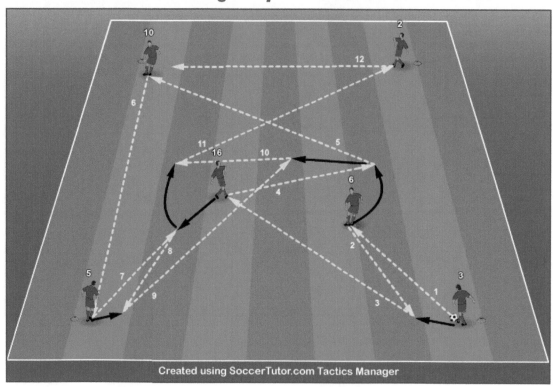

Created using SoccerTutor.com Tactics Manager

Objective
We practice switching play.

Description
In an area 25 x 25 yards, we have a switching play passing drill with a combination of 2 players in the middle (without turning with the ball).

The first player (3) passes to the closest player inside him (6). No.6 passes back, moves to provide a passing option and takes up the correct body shape to receive again. The third pass is directed to No.16 who is positioned further from the man in possession and makes a move to receive.

No.16 passes to No.6 who passes to the outside player positioned in the opposite corner (10). No.10 then passes to another outside player (in this occasion it is No.5). No.5 searches again for the closest player to make the first pass and the sequence of passes continues.

Coaching Points
1. The players should be constantly moving, timing their runs to the passes.
2. The correct body shape is needed to provide the necessary angles to make 1 touch passes.

PROGRESSION

2. Switching Play 3v3 (+3) Possession Game

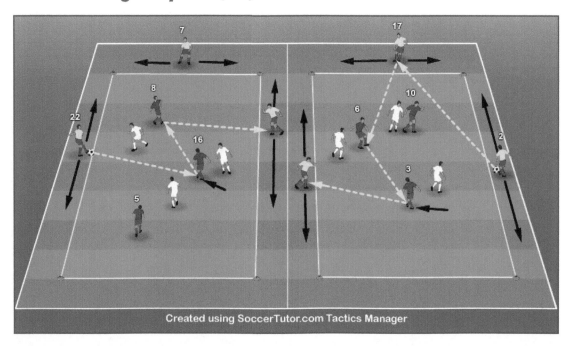

Created using SoccerTutor.com Tactics Manager

Objective

We practice switching play.

Description

We have 2 marked out areas of 15 X 25 yards in which 2 sets of players play the same small sided game with the same objective. There are 3v3 situations inside with 3 neutral players (1 at the top and 2 at the sides). Their aim is to retain possession and switch play from one neutral side player to the other (1 point).

The top neutral player helps the teams to achieve their aims but they are not allowed to pass to the other neutrals. The players in possession can pass the ball back to the neutral player who they received from in order to retain possession.

The players in possession have to complete at least 1 pass between themselves before they switch play in order to score a point.

The players inside the area are limited to 2 touches and the neutrals are limited to 1 touch (or pass within 3 seconds of receiving).

Coaching Points

1. The players should be constantly moving and have good quality in their passing.
2. Correct body shape (open up on the half turn) and positioning is important to view where the next pass goes.

PROGRESSION

3. 6v6 (+4) Position Specific Switching Play Dynamic Game

Created using SoccerTutor.com Tactics Manager

Objective

We practice switching play.

Description

In an area 30 x 40 yards, we play a dynamic 6v6 possession game with 4 additional outside players who play with the team in possession.

The red team aim to retain possession and move the ball from one side player to the other with the help of the outside players at the top (7 & 17). Their aim is to complete 2-3 consecutive switches of play in order to score a point.

If the whites win the ball, they look to dribble the ball through the end line. The red players can pass the ball back to the outside player who they received from in order to keep possession.

The red players inside use 2 touches and they have to complete at least 2 passes between themselves before they can move the ball to the opposite side. The outside players are not allowed to pass directly to other outside players and are limited to 1 touch or pass within 3 seconds of receiving.

Coaching Point

The players should always be aware to retain the team's balance and shape.

PROGRESSION

4. Switching Play Game with Divided Pitch & Side Zones

Created using SoccerTutor.com Tactics Manager

Objective

We work on switching play.

Description

2 teams play an 11v11 game where the pitch is divided in 2 to represent a strong side and a weak side. There are also 2 zones near the sidelines exclusively for the full backs of the red team.

The full backs inside this area can only use 2 touches and each time they receive a pass, the red team then has to switch play towards the weak side in order to have the right to shoot on goal.

If the whites win the ball, there are no restrictions in regards to the zones. The red team has to achieve a switch of play at least once before they can shoot at goal.

Coaching Points

1. The players need constant mobility and quality passing (well timed and weighted).

2. Correct body shape (open up on the half turn) and positioning is important to view where the next pass goes.

3. The players should always be aware to retain the team's balance and shape.

ATTACKING TACTICAL SITUATION 15

Switching Play Towards the Flanks Using Long Balls

ANALYSIS

SWITCHING PLAY TOWARDS THE FLANKS USING LONG BALLS

Created using SoccerTutor.com Tactics Manager

Analysis

In situations when Barcelona faced a team which used a compact formation and many of its players used to take up positions around the ball zone, the team used long ball towards players who created width on the flanks.

These players were either the wingers or the full backs who moved into advanced positions. By using this strategy, Barca could move the ball to the flanks before the defending team were able to react and shift across.

The basic elements for successfully using this strategy is the ability of the players to read the tactical situation, the accuracy of the long balls, as well as the supporting runs from the players on the flanks in order to create numerical advantages.

In this example, No.6 plays a long pass towards No.7 who provides width.

No.22 takes advantage of the transmission phase and as soon as No.17 receives, he is ready to move into a more advanced position and create a 2v1 situation on the left flank (with 7).

SESSION FOR THIS TACTICAL SITUATION
(4 PRACTICES)
1. Switching Play with Accurate Long Passes

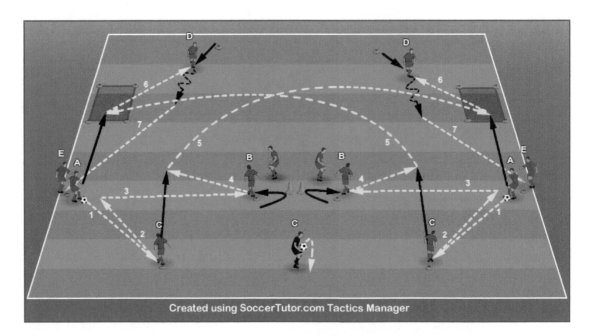

Created using SoccerTutor.com Tactics Manager

Objective
We practice switching play by using long passes.

Description
In an area 50 x 40 yards, this drill is executed on both sides at the same time.

The coach throws a ball up in the air. As soon as the ball hits the ground, player A passes to C who passes straight back. The next pass is directed to player B who has already checked away from the traffic cone while player C moves forward.

Player B passes to C who makes a long pass to player A on the other side inside the blue area. Player A times his run in order to receive on the move. Player A passes to D who drops back at the right moment, takes a first touch and passes to the starting point (player E).

The players move into the next position (A to B, B to etc). The size of the blue area depends on the level of the players.

Coaching Points
1. The correct weight and accuracy in the short and long passing is key in this exercise.
2. The player receiving the lofted pass should utilise all parts of the body to maximise control.

PROGRESSION

2. 4v2 (+3) / 4v2 (+3) Switching Play From Zone to Zone

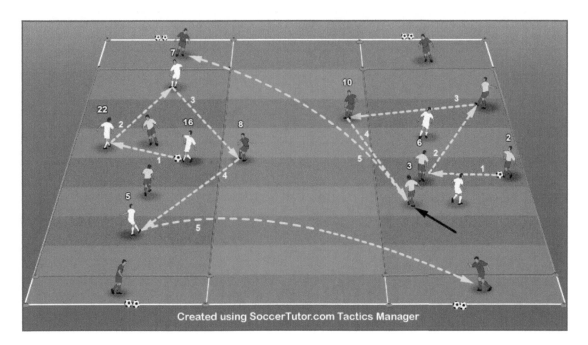

Created using SoccerTutor.com Tactics Manager

Objective
We practice switching play using long passes.

Description
In an area 45 x 20 yards, we have 3 teams of 6. There is a 4v2 situation inside the 2 side zones (15 x 20 yards) with 2 red outside players who help the teams of 4 to keep possession.

There are also 4 red outside players who are the target players inside the 4 small zones beside the 2 playing areas.

The teams of 4 switch play after completing at least 3 passes by making an accurate long pass towards the red target players.

When a switch is achieved, an outside player plays a new ball into the playing area. The 2 defenders try to prevent the switch by winning the ball and keeping it for as long as possible.

In this competitive game the teams of 4 try to achieve as many switches as possible within 3 minutes in order to win the competition.

Only the accurate long balls which are successfully controlled within the target players area count as a switch. The teams of 4 play with 2 touches while the outside players use 1 touch.

PROGRESSION

3. Switching Play Game with Divided Pitch & Side Zones (2)

Created using SoccerTutor.com Tactics Manager

Objective

We practice switching play using long passes.

Description

We have an 8v8 situation inside the playing area which is split into 2. There are also 2 blue zones near the sidelines in which only the red team's full backs are allowed. Inside these zones, the full backs can only use 2 touches.

The defensive midfielder and centre midfielder of the red team (wearing yellow bibs) can move freely across both areas.

The game starts with the goalkeeper who passes towards one of the 2 sides and the reds complete at least 2 passes before they can make a long pass towards the opposite side (blue side zone) and then try to score without any restrictions. The red full back on the weak side moves into the blue area and waits for the switch of play. As soon as this player receives and passes to a teammate, he should move out again.

If the whites win the ball, all players are free to move across all zones. If the reds win it back, they pass back to their goalkeeper and start a new attack. The red team has to achieve a switch of play every time they have possession.

Coaching Points

1. The players should take up the correct positions and distances in their support play.

2. When the player changes the direction of play, the pass must be accurate and be played for the full back to run onto.

PROGRESSION

4. Switching Play with 2v1s on the Flank 3 Zone Game

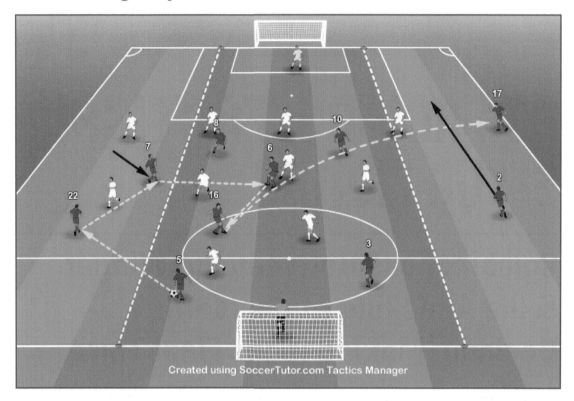

Created using SoccerTutor.com Tactics Manager

Objective

We practice switching play using long passes.

Description

2 teams play 11v11 in 2/3 of the pitch with 3 zones (as shown). When the red team moves the ball into one of the side zones, the white team are then not allowed to have have more than 1 player inside the other side zone. However, as soon as the ball is moved out of the first area, the whites can then move to enter the opposite zone to defend.

The red team aim to quickly switch the play with a long ball to take advantage of the 2v1 situation and score a goal. If the whites win the ball, all players can then move freely across all zones.

The red team should achieve at least 1 switch of play every time they have possession. However, if after the switch of play the team are unable to take advantage of the situation, they can then search for another way to attack.

Coaching Points

1. The emphasis here is on quick switches of play.

2. The players should play quick combinations to advantage of the numerical superiority on the flanks.

3. The accuracy of the long passing should be monitored.

ATTACKING TACTICAL SITUATION 16

Combinations Between the Winger & the Attacking Midfielder: Decision Making in the Final Third

ANALYSIS

COMBINATIONS BETWEEN THE WINGER & THE ATTACKING MIDFIELDER: DECISION MAKING IN THE FINAL THIRD

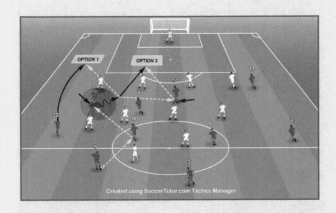

Situation 1

The winger (7) drops back to receive, while the full back (22) moves forward in a coordinated movement. This action either creates space down the flank or allows No.7 to receive unmarked.

The white full back does not follow No.7's movement as he drops deep so he does not leave to much space for No.22.

So No.7 receives unmarked, turns to face the opposition's goal and has 2 potential passing options (as shown in the diagram).

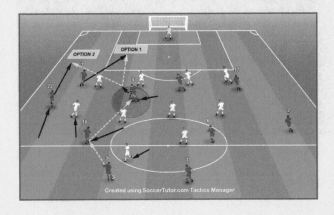

Situation 2

No.8 is the player who moves in behind the midfield line this time.

He receives unmarked as the centre back does not move to contest him, as he is aware that it would create space for No.10 or No.7 to exploit.

No.8 can turn and pass to No.7 in behind (option 1) or to No.22 who takes advantage of the free space on the flank, created by No.7 (option 2).

Analysis

When Barcelona managed to pass the ball to a player in behind the opposition's midfield line, the team could then reach the third stage of attack.

During the third stage, the players used good movements, collaborations and intelligent decision making to pick the best of the potential passing options.

SESSION FOR THIS TACTICAL SITUATION
(2 PRACTICES)
1. Combination Play in the Final Third

Created using SoccerTutor.com Tactics Manager

Objective

We practice combination play during the third stage of attack.

Description

We use an area 50 yards x 40 yards split into 2 areas as we run 2 passing combinations between the winger and the attacking midfielder dropping deep to receive.

On the left, player A (defensive midfielder) passes to C (attacking midfielder) as soon as he gets free of marking with an up and down move touching the blue cone. C plays the pass back and the next pass is directed to player B (winger) who drops back at t he right moment, receives and turns.

In the meantime, C has touched the red cone and moved towards B to provide a passing option. After a 1-2 combination, B shoots at goal. A moves to B's position, B to C and C towards the right side.

On the right, player A passes to C (winger) as soon as he gets free of marking and then receives the pass back. The next pass is directed to B (attacking midfielder) who drops back, receives, turns and plays a diagonal pass to C who shots on goal. A moves to B's position, B to C and C towards the left side.

PROGRESSION

2. Decision Making 3v2 Zonal Play with Finishing

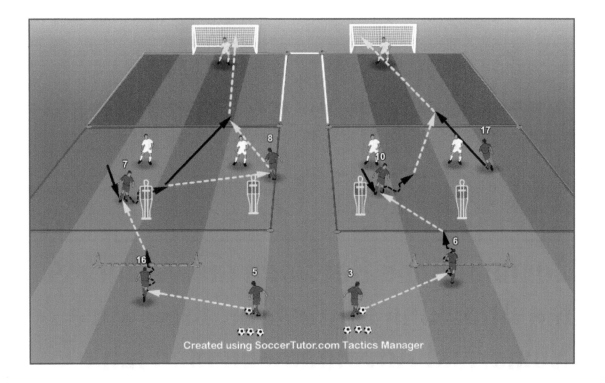

Created using SoccerTutor.com Tactics Manager

Objective

We practice combination play during the third stage of attack.

Description

The 2 combinations used in the previous drill between the winger and the attacking midfielder are now executed against 2 passive defenders using half a full size pitch.

The centre midfielders (16 and 6) receives from the centre back, moves forward through the red cones and passes to the attacking midfielder or the winger who drop back to receive unmarked behind the mannequins and turn towards the opposition's goal.

If the whites drop back to prevent the through pass, the man in possession can take advantage of the free space to dribble forward and take a shot.

The white players are told not to follow the forwards deep movements and leave them unmarked to turn. They also do not follow them beyond the blue area.

Coaching Points

1. The players need to be able to read the tactical situation.
2. The final pass needs to be well timed and weighted for the run in behind the defenders.
3. Stress the importance of accuracy in the finishing.

ATTACKING TACTICAL SITUATION 17

Combinations Between the Winger & the Attacking Midfielder: Creating a Numerical Advantage on the Flank

ANALYSIS

COMBINATIONS BETWEEN THE WINGER & THE ATTACKING MIDFIELDER: CREATING A NUMERICAL ADVANTAGE ON THE FLANK

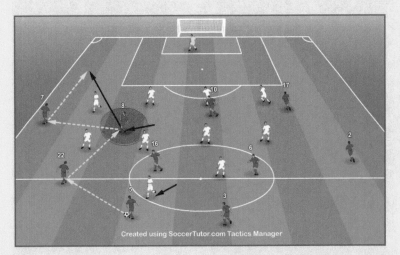

Situation 3

The attacking midfielder (8) receives behind the midfield line and passes to No.7 who is positioned near the sideline.

No.8 then makes a diagonal run to receive in behind the full back to create a 2v1 situation high up on the flank.

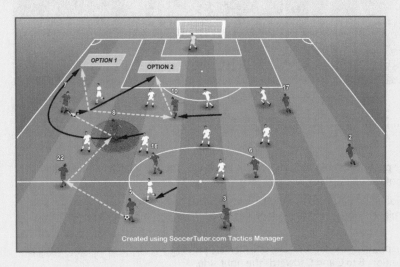

Situation 4

No.8 receives, passes to No.7 who is positioned high on the flank and then makes an overlapping run.

A 2v1 situation is created again and the new man in possession has 2 passing options.

SESSION FOR THIS TACTICAL SITUATION
(2 PRACTICES)
1. Quick Combination Play on the Flank

Created using SoccerTutor.com Tactics Manager

Objective
We practice combination play during the third stage of attack.

Description
In an area 50 x 40 yards, we have 2 passing combinations between the winger and the attacking midfielder, aiming to create a numerical advantage on the flank.

On the left, player A (defensive midfielder) passes to C (winger) who gets free of marking and receives the pass back. The next pass is directed to player B (attacking midfielder) who moves towards the ball carrier at the right moment, receives and turns.

B passes to C and makes the overlapping run. C dribbles the ball inside, passes to B and moves to receive the low cross and score. A moves to B's position, B to C and C towards the right side.

On the right, player A passes to C who makes the up and down movement to get free of marking and passes back to A. The next pass is directed to B who receives and turns. He passes to C and makes a diagonal run behind the mannequin and towards the sideline. C passes to B and moves to receive the low cross. A moves to B's position, B to C and C towards the left side.

PROGRESSION

2. Decision Making 3v2 Zonal Play with Finishing (2)

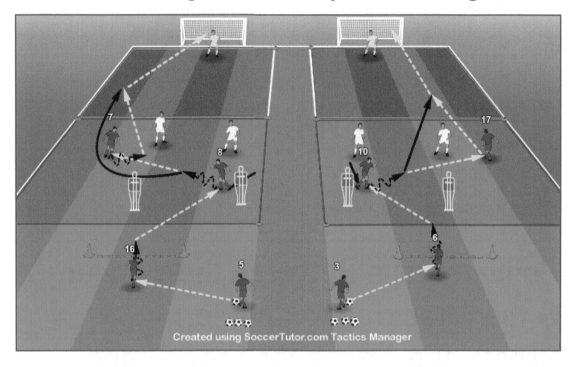

Created using SoccerTutor.com Tactics Manager

Objective

We practice combination play during the third stage of attack.

Description

The 2 combinations used in the previous drill between the winger and the attacking midfielder are now executed against 2 defenders who defend passively.

The 2 red forwards use the 2 combinations in synchronisation to create superiority in numbers on the flank and score. The 2 white defenders are not allowed to move beyond the blue area.

The centre midfielder (16 and 6) receives from the centre back, moves forward through the red cones and passes to the attacking midfielder who makes a move to receive behind the 2 mannequins. The 2 red players aim to create a numerical advantage on the flank and score.

The white defenders follow the attacking midfielders' movement and space is created towards the inside for the man in possession (winger) to take advantage of.

Coaching Points

1. The player receiving should do so on the half turn to quickly turn to face his opponents.
2. The overlapping run should begin as soon as the player has made his pass.
3. Accuracy of the shot is important, and not the power.

ATTACKING TACTICAL SITUATION 18

Combinations Between the Winger & the Attacking Midfielder: Create and Attack the Free Space

ANALYSIS

COMBINATIONS BETWEEN THE WINGER & THE ATTACKING MIDFIELDER: CREATE AND ATTACK THE FREE SPACE

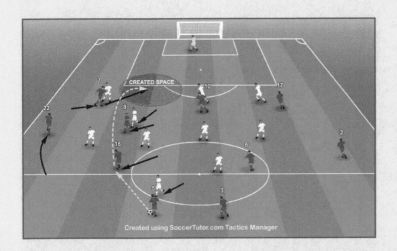

Situation 5

The attacking midfielder (8) drops back and moves in behind the white midfield line. The white centre back follows his movement.

This creates space for No.7 who moves to take advantage of the gap left in the middle.

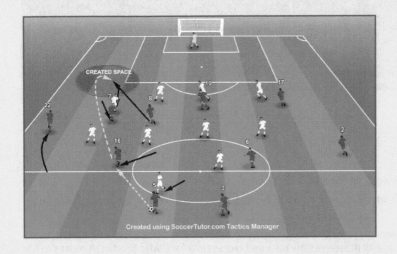

Situation 6

The winger No (7) drops back to receive.

The white full back follows this movement and space is created on the flank.

This time, No.8 moves to take advantage of the space in behind the full back on the flank.

SESSION FOR THIS TACTICAL SITUATION
(3 PRACTICES)
1. One-Two, Attack the Free Space, Cross and Finish

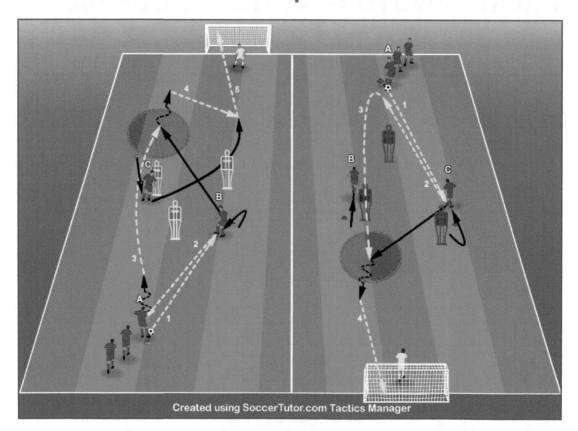

Created using SoccerTutor.com Tactics Manager

Objective

We practice combination play during the third stage of attack.

Description

We have another variation of the previous similar drills here.

On the left, player A (defensive midfielder) passes to B (attacking midfielder) who gets free of marking with an up and down movement.

B passes back and as soon as A receives the pass, player C (winger) drops back to receive and thus creates space on the flank. B moves to take advantage of it, receives the pass and crosses low for C who finishes. A moves to B's position, B to C and C towards the right side.

On the right, player A passes to C who gets free of marking. C passes back and as soon as A receives the pass, B drops back to receive and thus creates space in the centre. C receives the long ball behind the mannequin and shoots on goal. A moves to B, B to C and C towards the left side.

PROGRESSION

2. Create and Attack the Free Space in a 3v2 Zone

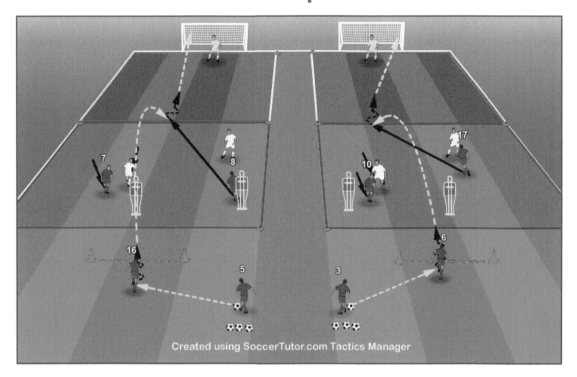

Created using SoccerTutor.com Tactics Manager

Objective

We practice combination play during the third stage of attack.

Description

We have a variation of the similar previous drills. The 2 combinations used in the previous drill between the winger and the attacking midfielder are now executed against 2 defenders who are told to follow the forward's movements in order for space to be created.

The red players have to be aware of the space created and move to take advantage of it. The white players use passive defending and are not allowed to follow the reds beyond the blue area.

The defensive midfielder (16 and 6) receives from the centre back, moves forward through the red cones and passes towards the free space created either by the winger or the attacking midfielder.

The 2 red players aim to attack the free space and score.

Coaching Points

1. The synchronised movements are the focus here. As one player drops back, the other moves forward to attack the space created.

2. The players need to display quality passing (well timed and weighted) and accuracy in their finishing.

PROGRESSION

3. 5v4 (+1) Position Specific 3 Zone Combination Game

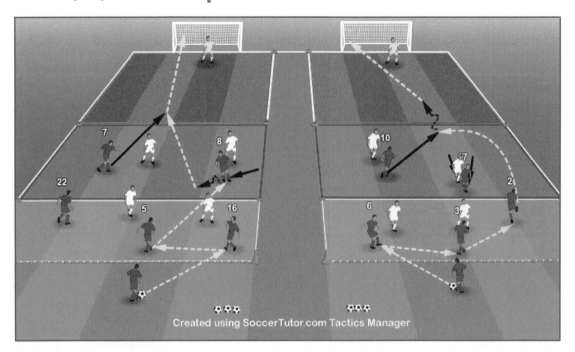

Created using SoccerTutor.com Tactics Manager

Objective

We work with the wingers and attacking midfielders who use various combinations in order to break through the opposition's defence.

Description

We have 2 small sided games using half a full size pitch. There are 3 areas which can be used to train any of the previous 6 situations analysed. The red players assess the tactical situation and try to use the appropriate combination to break through the defence.

Inside the white area, the 2 teams play 3(+1)v2 and inside the blue area there is a 2v2. Players must stay in their areas. The 3 red players in the white area use 2 touches (outside player has 1 touch) and they aim to pass the ball to their teammates in the blue area.

The 2 red players inside the blue area receive, combine and try to break through the defence to score. They can either dribble the ball through the red line or receive beyond it with the offside rule in action. The white players are not allowed in the red area.

If the whites win the ball, they seek to dribble the ball through the red end line. If this happens, players can move freely across all zones. If the reds win possession back, they should pass the ball to the outside player in order for the game to start again.

Coaching Points

1. The players should be aware to always retain the balance of the team.

2. Players need to read the tactical situation, be constantly mobile and use synchronised movements.

ATTACKING TACTICAL SITUATION 19

Combinations Between the Winger & the Attacking Midfielder: Overloading the Side in the Third Stage of Attack

ANALYSIS

COMBINATIONS BETWEEN THE WINGER & THE ATTACKING MIDFIELDER: OVERLOADING THE SIDE IN THE THIRD STAGE OF ATTACK

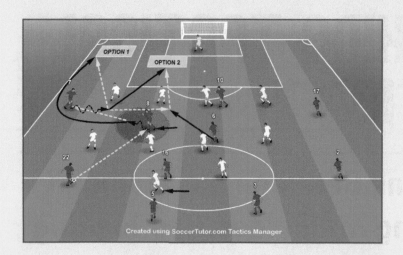

Situation 7

No.8 receives unmarked from a pass by the left back.

No.8 passes to No.7 on the flank and makes an overlapping run.

No.7 dribbles inside and has 2 available options. He can either pass to No.8 on the flank (option 1) or combine with No.6 who has moved to overload the side (option 2).

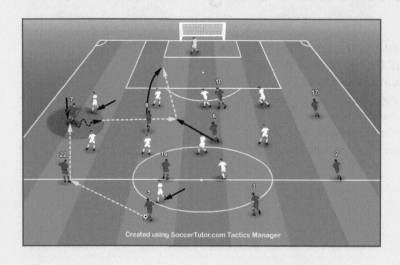

Situation 8

No.7 drops back, receives and dribbles inside.

No.8 makes the forward run, while No.6 moves towards the strong side to overload the side and provide a passing option.

The ball ends up with No.8 through on goal after a pass from No.6.a

SESSION FOR THIS TACTICAL SITUATION
(4 PRACTICES)
1. Overloading the Side Pattern of Play

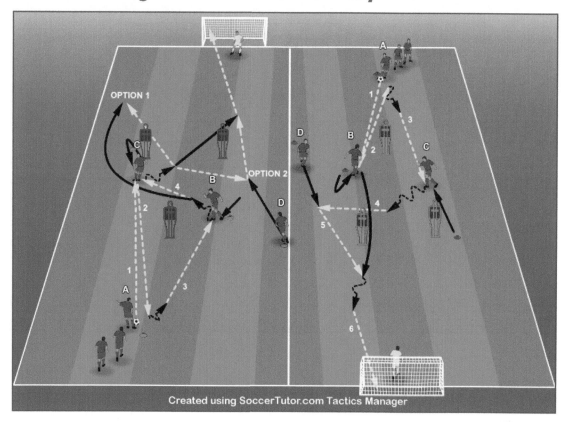

Created using SoccerTutor.com Tactics Manager

Objective

We practice combinations during the third stage of attack after overloading the side.

Description

This is a variation of similar previous drills with the focus on overloading one side.

On the left, player A (defensive midfielder) passes to C (winger) who gets free of marking with an up and down movement. D passes back and as soon as A receives the pass, player B (attacking midfielder) drops back to receive. B turns, passes to C and makes the overlapping run. C dribbles inside and has 2 options, to pass to B or to combine with D.

A moves to B's position, B to C, C to D and D towards the right side.

On the right, player A passes to B who gets free of marking. B passes back and as soon as A receives the pass, C drops back to receive and dribbles inside while B makes a movement towards the free space (3rd man run). The ball ends up with B through D.

A moves to B's position, B to C, C to D and D towards the left side.

VARIATION

2. Overloading the Side 3v2 Zonal Play with Finishing

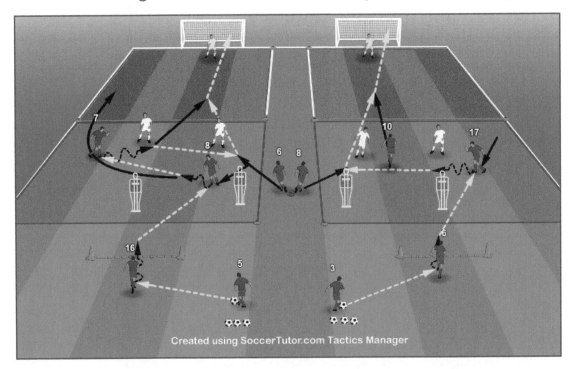

Created using SoccerTutor.com Tactics Manager

Objective

We practice combination play during the third stage of attack.

Description

The combinations used in the previous drill between the winger and the attacking midfielder are now executed against 2 defenders who are told to defend passively and are not allowed beyond the blue area.

There are 2 extra players (attacking midfielders) positioned on the blue cone and they enter the playing area at the right moment.

The defensive midfielders (16 and 6) receive from the centre back, move forward through the red cones and either pass to the winger or the attacking midfielder.

The 2 red players, helped by the second attacking midfielder who enters the playing area at the right moment and overloads the side, aim to break through the defence and score.

Coaching Points

1. As one player drops back to receive, the other should be moving into an available passing lane.

2. The player receiving the first pass into the blue area should do so on the half turn, so he can quickly face his opponents and combine with his teammate.

PROGRESSION

3. 6v4 (+1) Position Specific 3 Zone Combination Game

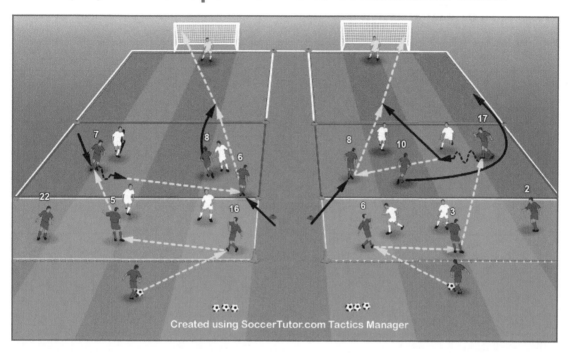

Created using SoccerTutor.com Tactics Manager

Objective

We work with the wingers and attacking midfielders with the aim to use various combinations in order to break through the opposition's defence.

Description

This is a variation of a similar previous drill.

Inside the white area, the 2 teams play 3(+1) v2 and 2v2 in the blue area. There are also 2 red players outside the areas (6 and 8) who enter the blue areas when the ball is passed in there. The white players must stay in their areas.

The 3 red players inside the white area use 2 touches (outside player uses 1 touch) and aim to pass the ball to their teammates in the blue area.

The 2 red players inside the blue area seek to receive, combine and break through the opposition's defence by dribbling the ball through the red line or receiving beyond it to score.

If the whites win the ball, they aim to dribble the ball through the red end line. If this happens, the players can move freely across all zones. If the reds win the ball back, they pass to the outside player for the game to re-start.

Coaching Points

1. Correct body shape (open up on the half turn) and positioning is important to view where the next pass goes.
2. The players should always be aware to retain the team's balance.

PROGRESSION

4. Combinations Between the Winger & the Attacking Midfielder Final Game

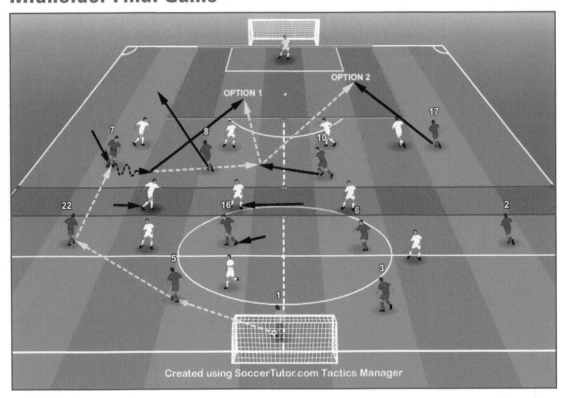

Objective

We work with the wingers, the attacking midfielders and the full backs with the aim to use various combinations in order to break through the opposition's defence and score.

Description

The 2 teams play an 11v11 game. The pitch is divided in half (right and left) and only the white striker and the red attacking midfielders can move across both sides.

Inside the low zone, the teams play 3v2 or 3v1 on each side (depending on the positioning of the striker). The red players try to find a way to pass the ball to their teammates inside the high zone where there is a 2v2 situation on each side. 3 opposition midfielders play inside the blue area and try to block the passes towards the players inside the high zone. They must stay within this zone.

When the ball is played into the high zone, a player can move across to the strong side to create a numerical advantage (3v2). Only the 4 forwards and the 4 white defenders can go in the penalty area. If the whites win the ball, they counter attack and all players can move freely across all zones.

Coaching Point

The wingers and attacking midfielders should demonstrate all the different combinations they have been practicing here in this final game.

ATTACKING TACTICAL SITUATION 20

Combinations Between the Winger, the Full Back and the Attacking Midfielder: Create and Attack the Free Space on the Flank

ANALYSIS

COMBINATIONS BETWEEN THE WINGER, THE FULL BACK AND THE ATTACKING MIDFIELDER: CREATE AND ATTACK THE FREE SPACE ON THE FLANK

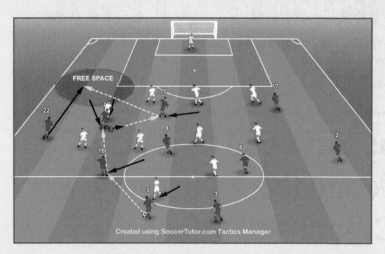

Situation 9

No.7 makes a well coordinated movement together with No.22.

No.7 drops back and No.22 moves forward.

The white full back follows No.7 and space is created on the flank. No.22 receives the ball in behind through No.10.

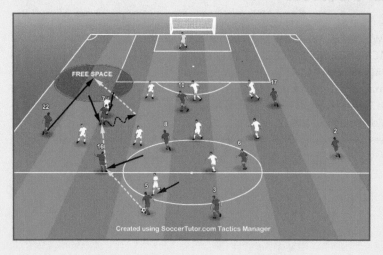

Situation 10

No.7 and No22 move in the same way again.

This time, No.7 receives and passes directly to No.22 after dribbling inside.

SESSION FOR THIS TACTICAL SITUATION
(4 PRACTICES)
1. Create Space, Receive, Turn and Attacking Combination

Created using SoccerTutor.com Tactics Manager

Objective

We practice combination play during the third stage of attack.

Description

In an area 50 x 40 yards (split into 2 halves) there are 2 combinations between the winger, the attacking midfielder and the full back aiming to attack the free space on the flank.

On the left, player A (defensive midfielder) passes to C (winger) who gets free of marking with an up and down movement, creating space for the full back. C turns in the blue area and passes to D (attacking midfielder). D makes a pass into the space on the flank for B (full back). B moves forward and crosses low for player D. A moves to B's position, B to C, C to D and D towards the right side.

On the right, player A passes to C who turns within the blue area and passes to B. B moves forward and crosses low for D to score. A moves to B's position, B to C, C to D and D towards the left side.

Coaching Points

1. The player in the blue square needs to take a directional first touch to quickly make the transition for a pass to their teammate.

2. This exercise is all about timing as the players need to synchronise their movements.

PROGRESSION

2. Creating and Attacking Free Space Zonal Play with Finishing

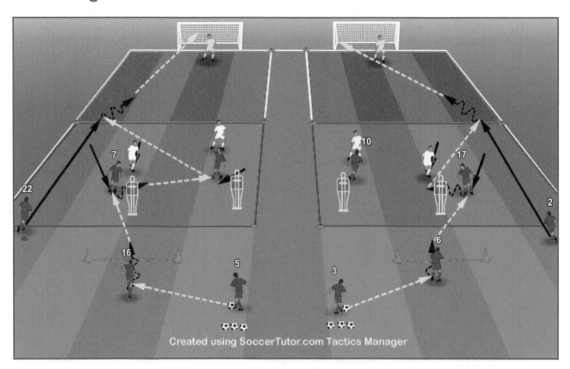

Created using SoccerTutor.com Tactics Manager

Objective

We practice combination play during the third stage of attack.

Description

The 2 combinations used in the previous drill between the winger, the full back and the attacking midfielder are now executed against 2 passive defenders who are told to follow the forwards as they drop deep.

The 2 white defenders are not allowed in the red area.

The centre midfielders (16 and 6) receive from the centre backs, move forward through the red cones and pass to the winger who drops back and receives behind the mannequin.

The winger creates space for the red full back as the white full back is told to follow the winger's movement. The 3 red players attack the free space on the flank and try to score.

Coaching Points

1. The players need to be aware, read the tactical situation and use synchronised movements.
2. There should be a high quality in turning, passing and finishing.

PROGRESSION

3. 5v4 (+1) Position Specific 3 Zone Combination Game

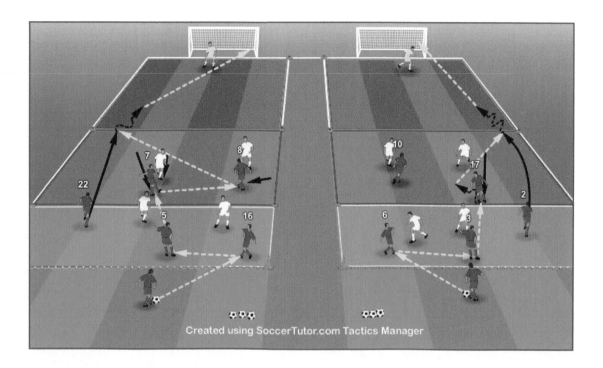

Created using SoccerTutor.com Tactics Manager

Objective

We work with the wingers, the attacking midfielders and the full backs, using various combinations in order to break through the opposition's defence.

Description

This is a variation of the previous drill with 3 areas.

This time the red full backs are allowed to enter the blue area in order to take advantage of the created space.

Coaching Points

1. The correct body shape should be monitored (opening up) and receiving/passing with the back foot (foot furthest away from the ball).

2. The players need to be aware to always retain the team's balance.

PROGRESSION

4. Combinations Between the Wingers, the Attacking Midfielder and the Full Backs Final Game

Created using SoccerTutor.com Tactics Manager

Objective

We work with the wingers, the attacking midfielders and the full backs, using various combinations in order to break through the opposition's defence and score.

Description

The 2 teams play an 11v11 game. The pitch is divided in half (right and left) and only the white striker can move across both sides.

Inside the low zone, the teams play 3v2 or 3v1 on each side (depending on the positioning of the striker). The red players try to find a way to pass the ball to their teammates inside the high zone where there is a 2v2 situation on each side.

3 opposition midfielders play inside the blue area and try to block the passes towards the players inside the high zone. They must stay within this zone.

The red fullbacks are free to enter the high zone in order to create a numerical advantage (3v2) and take advantage of the free space by using well timed runs. If the whites win the ball, they counter attack and all players can move freely across all zones.

ATTACKING TACTICAL SITUATION 21

Retaining Balance During the Attacking Phase Using a 2 Man Defence

ANALYSIS

RETAINING BALANCE DURING THE ATTACKING PHASE USING A 2 MAN DEFENCE

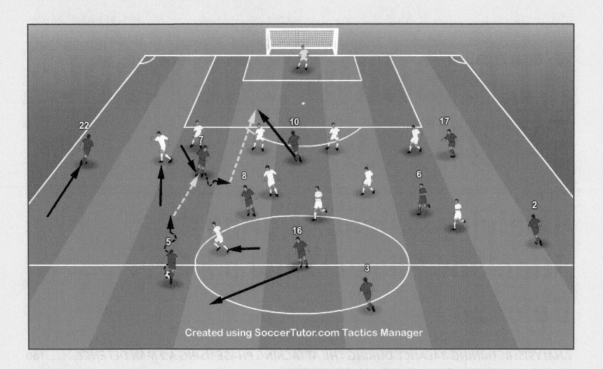

Created using SoccerTutor.com Tactics Manager

Analysis

When Barcelona used a 2 man defence during the build up phase and one of them decided to move forward, the defensive midfielder (Busquets - 16) would move back to provide cover and retain the team's balance.

In the example shown here, as soon as No.5 moves forward with the ball, No.16 moves back to cover his position and retain the team's balance.

SESSION FOR THIS TACTICAL SITUATION
(4 PRACTICES)
1. Passing, Moving & Retaining Balance with 2 Defenders

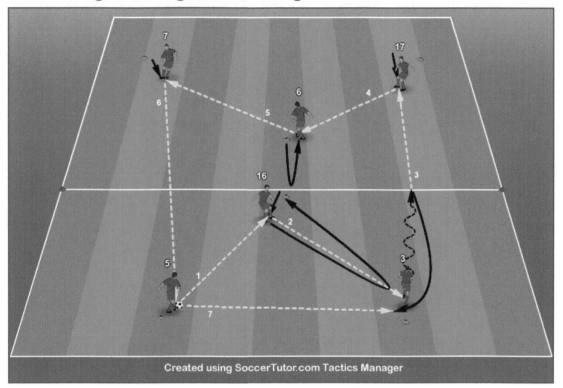

Created using SoccerTutor.com Tactics Manager

Objective

We work on retaining balance at the back when using a 2 man defence.

Description

In an area 25 x 25 yards, we work with 2 centre backs, 1 defensive midfielder, 1 centre midfielder and 2 wingers.

Player No.5 starts the drill by passing to No.16 who receives and passes back to No.3. No.3 moves forward with the ball and No16 moves back to take up his position. No.6 then drops back to take up No.16's position.

As soon as the man in possession dribbles the ball up to the white line, he passes to No.17 who drops back at the right moment to receive. No.17 passes to No.6 and No.6 passes to No.7. No.7 passes back to No.5 and No.3 returns to his starting position in time to receive again.

The final pass is from No.5 to No.3. All players return to their starting positions and the players run the drill to the other side with No.5 moving forward with the ball.

Coaching Points

1. The accuracy and weight of the pass needs to be correct.

2. The rhythm and timing of the movement together with the pass is key.

3. Make sure the players communicate with their teammates and heads are up.

PROGRESSION

2. Covering the Centre Back's Forward Run with the Ball

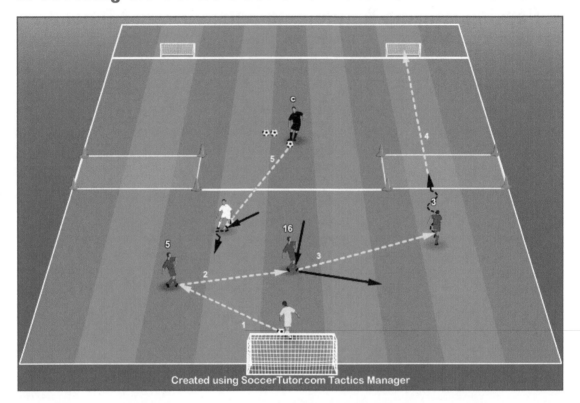

Created using SoccerTutor.com Tactics Manager

Objective

We work on retaining balance at the back when using a 2 man defence.

Description

In an area 25 x 25 yards, the red team have a 3v1 advantage inside the low zone. The goalkeeper passes the ball to one of the centre backs (3 or 5) and the red defenders try to overcome the white forward's passive pressure.

1 red player has to dribble into the white zone and shoot into the mini goal.

At the same time, the defensive midfielder tries to keep the team balanced by taking up the position of the defender who has moved forward.

As soon as the player in possession shoots, the coach passes a new ball towards the white player.

The red players have to react quickly and deal with the situation successfully to prevent him from scoring.

Coaching Point

The players need to be aware of the situation to quickly react to the changing circumstances.

PROGRESSION

3. Retaining Balance at the Back 2 Zone Small Sided Game

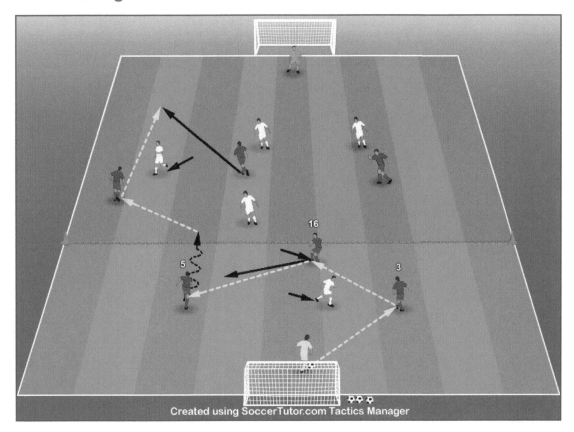

Created using SoccerTutor.com Tactics Manager

Objective

We work on retaining balance at the back when using a 2 man defence.

Description

In an area 25 x 25 yards, the red players have a 3v1 situation inside the low zone and there is a 3v4 situation in the high zone. This becomes 4v4 as soon as 1 of the red defenders dribbles the ball forward (as shown). Only 1 defender is allowed at a time.

The defensive midfielder (16) seeks to retain the team's balance as well by covering No.5 and maintaining a 2v1 situation, while the other red players try to score.

The whites try to win the ball and score themselves. If this happens, all players can then move freely across both zones. The red players then try to win the ball back as soon as possible. If they do, they pass the ball back to their goalkeeper so the centre back can get back and we start a new attack.

If the ball goes out of play, the game restarts with the red team's goalkeeper.

Coaching Points

1. The players should be able to fully exploit the superiority in numbers at the back.
2. Winning the ball back as soon as possible is one of the key elements of this exercise.

PROGRESSION

4. Retaining Balance at the Back with Building Up Play Game

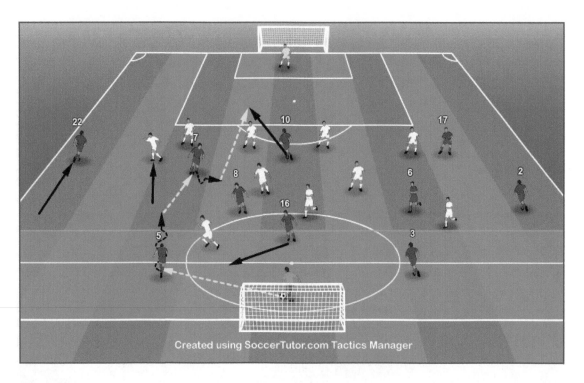

Created using SoccerTutor.com Tactics Manager

Objective

We work on retaining balance at the back when using a 2 man defence.

Description

2 teams play an 11v11 game. There is a 3v1 situation inside the low zone and a 7v9 situation in the high zone.

The red defenders have a numerical advantage and 1 defender dribbles the ball into the high zone to create an 8v9 situation in the high zone with the aim to score.

The defensive midfielder (16) moves to retain balance and keep superiority in numbers inside the low zone so they can win the ball back quickly after losing possession.

If the whites win the ball, they pass to their teammate inside the blue area trying to score as soon as possible and all players can move freely across zones. If the reds win the ball back again, they pass to their goalkeeper and the game restarts.

Only 1 red player can enter the high zone. The whites are not allowed to enter the blue area (low zone) unless they win possession.

ATTACKING TACTICAL SITUATION 22

Retaining Balance During the Attacking Phase Using a 3 Man Defence

ANALYSIS

RETAINING BALANCE DURING THE ATTACKING PHASE USING A 3 MAN DEFENCE

Created using SoccerTutor.com Tactics Manager

Analysis

The defensive midfielder (Busquets - 16) was the player who retained the team's balance in situations when the team used a 3 man defence during their build up play.

When one of the centre backs moved forward, Busquets moved back to provide cover and keep the team balanced.

In this example, No.3 (Pique) receives and moves forward with the ball. No.16 drops back to take up his position and retain the team's balance.

SESSION FOR THIS TACTICAL SITUATION
(4 PRACTICES)
1. Passing, Moving & Retaining Balance with 3 Defenders

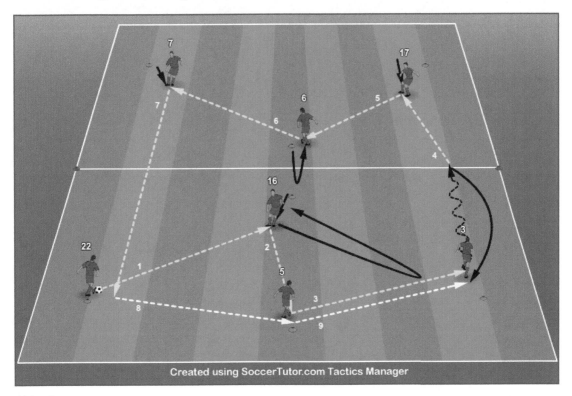

Created using SoccerTutor.com Tactics Manager

Objective

We work on retaining balance at the back when using a 3 man defence.

Description

In an area 30 x 30 yards, No.22 starts the drill by passing to the defensive midfielder (16) who passes to No.5. No.5 passes to No.3 who moves forward with the ball. At the same time, No.16 moves back to take up his position and No.6 drops back to take up No.16's position.

As soon as the man in possession dribbles the ball through up to white line, he passes to No.17 who drops back at the right moment to receive. No.17 passes to No.6 (who has moved back again) and passes to No.7. No.7 passes back to No.22 as No.3 returns to his starting position to be ready for the 9th and final pass.

When No16 sees that No3 returns to his position, he moves to his starting position too. After the final pass, the sequence is repeated towards the other side with No.22 being the defender who moves forward with the ball.

Coaching Points

1. The players need to have good awareness, e.g. moving to cover at the right time and moving forward again at the right time.

2. Accuracy of pass, weight of pass and good communication are all key elements for this practice.

PROGRESSION

2. Covering the Centre Back's Forward Run with the Ball (2)

Created using SoccerTutor.com Tactics Manager

Objective

We work on retaining balance at the back when using a 3 man defence.

Description

In an area 35 x 35 yards, the red players play 4v2 inside the low zone. The red defenders need to overcome the forward's passive pressure. No.22 becomes a third centre back here as the team use a 3 man defence.

1 defender can dribble forward with the ball into the white zones and score in the mini goals. At the same time, the defensive midfielder tries to keep the team balanced by taking up the position of the defender who has moved forward.

As soon as the player shoots, the coach passes a new ball towards the 2 white players. The red players have to react quickly to the 3v2 situation and prevent them from scoring.

Coaching Points

1. With a numerical advantage, there should easily be a man free to receive and move forward with the ball.

2. The players need quick reactions to the changing situations.

PROGRESSION

3. Retaining Balance at the Back 2 Zone Small Sided Game (2)

Objective

We work on retaining balance at the back when using a 3 man defence.

Description

In an area 35 x 45 yards, there is a 4v2 situation in the low zone and a 3v4 situation in the high zone.

This becomes 4v4 as soon as one of the red defenders dribbles the ball forward (as shown). Only 1 defender is allowed at a time.

The defensive midfielder (16) seeks to retain the team's balance as well as covering No.5 and maintaining a 3v2 situation while the other red players try to score.

The whites try to win the ball and score themselves. If this happens, all players can then move freely across both zones. The red players then try to win the ball back as soon as possible. If they do, they pass the ball back to their goalkeeper so the centre back can get back and we start a new attack.

If the ball goes out of play, the game restarts with the red team's goalkeeper.

PROGRESSION

4. Retaining Balance at the Back with Building Up Play Game (2)

Created using SoccerTutor.com Tactics Manager

Objective

We work on retaining balance at the back when using a 3 man defence.

Description

The 2 teams play an 11v11 game. There is a 4v2 situation in the low zone and a 6v8 situation in the high zone. 1 red defender can dribble the ball into the high zone as the reds try to score. The defensive midfielder (16) seeks to retain the team's balance and a numerical advantage in the low zone.

If the white players win the ball, they pass to their teammate inside the blue area (low zone) and try to score as soon as possible. When they win the ball, all players can move freely across the zones. If the reds win the ball back again, they pass it back to their goalkeeper and the game restarts.

Only 1 red defender can enter the high zone. The whites are not allowed to enter the blue area unless they win possession.

Coaching Points

1. The combination play should be at a high tempo to score as soon as possible.
2. The team should always retain superiority in numbers at the back to prepare for a negative transition.

ATTACKING TACTICAL SITUATION 23

Retaining Balance During the Attacking Phase: The Defensive Midfielder's Role

ANALYSIS

RETAINING BALANCE DURING THE ATTACKING PHASE: THE DEFENSIVE MIDFIELDER'S ROLE

Situation 1

Barcelona build up play using 2 players at the back. No.16 stays close to the defenders as the opposition plays with 2 forwards.

After No.5's pass, the white full back wins possession. No.8 (the safety player) moves to close him down. However, the man in possession manages to successfully pass to the forward.

The new player in possession is immediately put under pressure by No.16 and No.5 while No.3 is in a covering position.

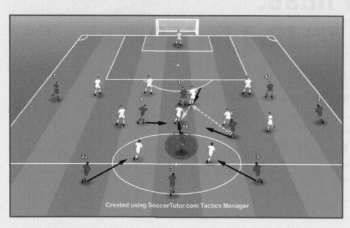

Situation 2

Here Barcelona use a 3 man defence, so No.16 is in a more advanced position.

When they lose possession, No.16 moves forward to put pressure on the ball as there is already a 3v2 situation at the back.

No.22 and No.3 mark the forwards and No.5 is in a covering position.

Analysis

The defensive midfielder not only provides cover to the forward moving defenders during the build up phase, but also had a very important role during the attacking phase.

In situations that Barca used 2 players at the back and the opposing team played with 2 forwards, No.16 played close to the defenders to create a 3v2 situation. If Barca used a 3 man defence in the same situation, No.16 could play in a more advanced position as there was already a 3v2 advantage at the back.

SESSION FOR THIS TACTICAL SITUATION
(3 PRACTICES)
1. Retaining Balance During the Attacking Phase with Zones

Created using SoccerTutor.com Tactics Manager

Objective

We work on retaining balance during the attacking phase by maintaining a numerical advantage at the back and preparing for the negative transition.

Description

In an area 30 x 40 yards, 2 teams play 4v4 inside the white large zone with 2 outside players for each team (as shown). Inside the blue area, there is a 3v2 (2 centre backs & 1 defensive midfielder v 2 forwards) and these players are free to move from area to area. The outside players use 1 touch.

The red players try to retain possession and complete 12- 15 passes using both the outside players and the players inside the blue area. The reds should always have a numerical advantage in the blue zone so they are prepared for a negative transition.

If the whites win the ball they pass to one of their teammates in the blue area with the aim of dribbling the ball through the end line (with the help of the white outside players). All the players can move freely across zones if the whites win the ball.

With players moving into the main area, the red defensive midfielder (16) is responsible for creating both equality in numbers inside the white area and superiority in numbers inside the blue one.

For instance. if 1 of the forwards enters the main area, No.16 should follow him to create equality in numbers (5v5) and superiority in numbers (2v1 inside the blue area). If both white players from the blue area enter the white area, No.16 and one of the centre backs should enter the white area too.

PROGRESSION

2. Retaining Balance: 2 Zone Negative Transition Game

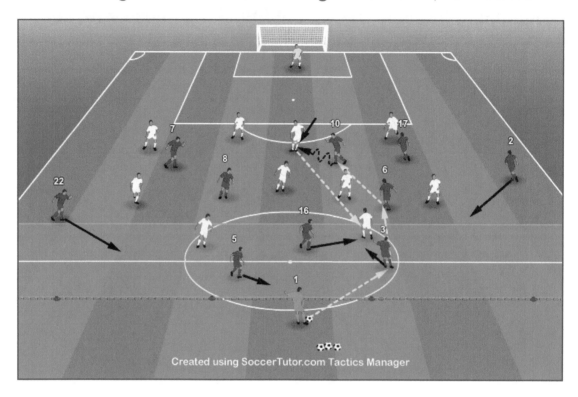

Created using SoccerTutor.com Tactics Manager

Objective

We work on retaining balance during the attacking phase by maintaining a numerical advantage at the back and preparing for the negative transition.

Description

2 teams play an 11v11 game with the red team's goalkeeper used as an outside player who helps his team retain possession and starts the practice. Inside the blue area, there are 2 centre backs and 1 defensive midfielder and 2 white forwards. These players can move freely from area to area.

The defensive midfielder's positioning is used to retain the superiority in numbers inside the main area when attacking. When the red team manages to shoot on goal, the game restarts with the red goalkeeper again.

If the whites win the ball, they aim to pass to their teammates in the blue area and dribble through the end line and all players can move freely (only when whites win possession). The red players must react quickly after losing possession and try to regain the ball back as soon as possible.

Coaching Points

1. Players need to read the tactical situation, always conscious to retain balance at the back.

2. Quick reactions are needed to respond after losing possession.

3. There needs to be good communication and collaboration between the players.

VARIATION

3. Retaining Balance: 2 Zone Negative Transition Game (2)

Created using SoccerTutor.com Tactics Manager

Objective

We work on retaining balance during the attacking phase by maintaining a numerical advantage at the back and preparing for the negative transition.

Description

2 teams play an 11v11 game. The red team's aim is to score, while the white players seek to win the ball and counter attack.

The defensive midfielder (16) makes sure the team retains a numerical advantage (3v2 or 2v1) in the blue area in order for his team to be able to react quickly after losing possession and win the ball back as soon as possible.

When the whites win possession all players can move freely across zones. The white team's formation is 4-4-2, but if they play 4-2-3-1, No.16 can play a few yards higher but always have it in mind to ensure superiority in numbers inside the marked area.

Coaching Points

1. Correct body shape (open up on the half turn) and positioning is important to view where the options for where the next pass is going.

2. Decision making is important; when to hold the ball, play a first time pass or dribble forwards.

3. The red team must be very alert to a potential transition from attack to defence and quickly pressure the ball carrier (getting bodies back behind the ball).

ATTACKING TACTICAL SITUATION 24

Retaining Balance During the Attacking Phase: The Full Back's Role

ANALYSIS

RETAINING BALANCE DURING THE ATTACKING PHASE: THE FULL BACK'S ROLE

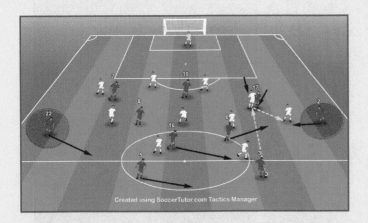

Situation 1

Both the full backs (22 and 2) have taken up balanced positions, so when possession is lost they can immediately move into effective defensive positions.

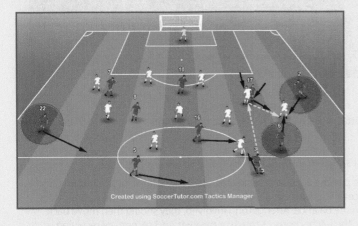

Situation 2

The full back (2) has left his balanced position and moved into a more advanced one. However, the attacking midfielder (6) has moved to provide cover and help retain the team's balance. So when possession is lost, No.6 can put immediate pressure on the ball and No.2 moves quickly back.

No.22 retains a balanced position and is able to take up a good defensive position.

Analysis

The positioning of Barcelona's full backs during the attacking phase was very important for the team, as without it, the retaining of the defensive balance could not be obtained.

In this example, the full backs retain balanced positions during the build up. This means that they had positions which enabled them to take up effective defensive positions against their direct opponents in case possession was lost. In cases when the full backs decided to leave these positions and move into more advanced positions, other players (e.g. the attacking midfielders) moved to cover for them. This meant the team could retain its balance all the time.

SESSION FOR THIS TACTICAL SITUATION
(3 PRACTICES)
1. Full Back's Decision Making in a 3 Zone Dynamic Game

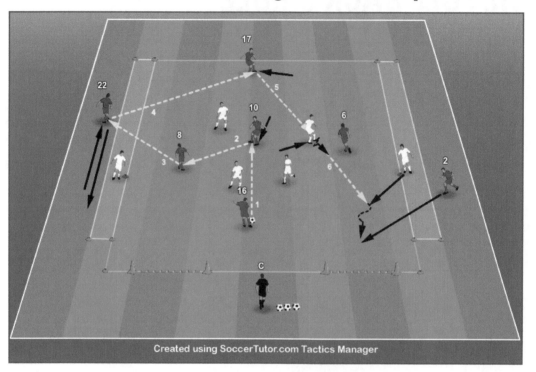

Created using SoccerTutor.com Tactics Manager

Objective

We work on retaining balance during the attacking phase by finding the right moment to move forward.

Description

2 teams play 5v4 inside an area 35 x 35 yards. There are also 2 zones on either side (5 x 30 yards).

The red players keep possession with the help of the 2 fullbacks who are outside and move forward when they feel that it is the right time. This should take place when the team has clear possession and the attacking midfielder should move to a covering position to retain the balance. After getting involved, they should then move back quickly and take up their balanced position. The full backs use 1 touch or pass within 3 seconds of receiving.

If the whites win the ball, they pass to the players on the blue cones that enter the area as soon as their teammates win possession. The aim is then to dribble the ball through the 1 of the 2 goals. If they are unable to do this, they simply help their team retain possession inside the main area.

Both white players can enter the blue area at the same time. The red full backs move inside to prevent the whites from scoring and help their team win the ball back, and if they do they pass to the coach for the game to restart.

Coaching Points

1. The players need to use well timed forward runs.
2. The team needs to have quick reactions, ready to respond to a possible negative transition.

PROGRESSION

2. Timing the Full Back's Runs in an 8v9 Dynamic SSG

Created using SoccerTutor.com Tactics Manager

Objective
We work on retaining balance during the attacking phase by finding the right moment to move forward.

Description
2 teams play an 8v8 in half a pitch.

The red team's full backs aim to find the right time to move forward without leaving the team unbalanced. The attacking midfielders also play an important role in keeping the team balanced as they have to sure to take up covering positions in cases if the full backs move into advanced positions.

If possession is lost, the red team try to win the ball back as high up the pitch as they can. The whites try to score in 1 of the 3 small goals, but must shoot within the red zone shown.

Coaching Points
1. Synchronised movements are needed, as in this example. The winger moves inside and the full back dribbles forward to exploit the space created.
2. Keeping the team balanced is important, so the players cover each other when their teammates move into advanced positions.
3. The defender who moves forward needs to wait for the right moment and dribble forward (attacking the free space).
4. Winning the ball high up the field will prevent the whites from entering the red zone with the ball.

PROGRESSION

3. Timing the Full Back's Runs in an 8v9 Dynamic SSG

Created using SoccerTutor.com Tactics Manager

Objective

We work on retaining balance during the attacking phase by finding the right moment to move forwards.

Description

2 teams play an 11 v 11 game in 2/3 of a pitch.

The red team's full backs wait for the right moment to move forward and enter the red area creating a 4v4 situation inside it and 2v1 on the flank.

In these situations, the attacking midfielders should move into covering positions in order to provide safety in case possession is lost.

The white team try to win the ball and counter attack. As soon as they win the ball, there are no restrictions and all players can move freely from zone to zone.

Only the red full backs can enter the red area. The white midfielders or forwards are not allowed, so the red attacking midfielders have a responsibility to keep the team balanced to limit problems for their team.

ATTACKING TACTICAL SITUATION 25

The Negative Transition

ANALYSIS

THE NEGATIVE TRANSITION

Created using SoccerTutor.com Tactics Manager

Analysis

Barcelona's main aim during the negative transition was the immediate regaining of possession. To achieve this there was always a safety player near the ball zone as well as a quick reaction from all the players.

The safety player would also have the appropriate position in order to apply immediate pressure on the ball by reducing the available time and space of the man in possession.

In this example, the safety player is No.6 who passes the ball to No.17. No17 receives but the opposition's midfielder contests him and wins possession.

No.6 (the safety player) then moves quickly to close him down and the other Barca players also react quickly to move towards the ball zone.

In order for the negative transition to be successful, all players should take part.

SESSION FOR THIS TACTICAL SITUATION
(4 PRACTICES)

1. 4v4 (+4) Quick Reactions Dynamic Negative Transition Game

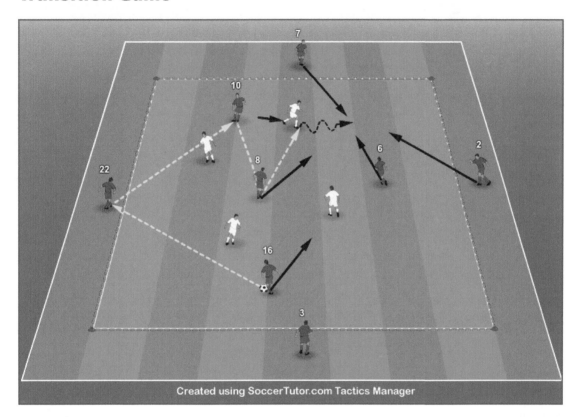

Created using SoccerTutor.com Tactics Manager

Objective

We work on quick reactions in the negative transition.

Description

In an area 30 x 30 yards, there is a 4v4 situation. The red team retain possession with the help of the outside players, while the white players try to win the ball and then dribble it through 1 of the 4 sides.

There can be an aim for the red team to complete a certain amount of passes in order to win a point.

When possession is lost, the outside players enter the marked area and together with the inside players try to regain possession before the white players manage to dribble the ball through the lines.

The red players inside use 2 touches while the red outside players play with 1 touch.

Coaching Point

The players need to be aware and have quick reactions after losing possession.

PROGRESSION

2. 5v5 (+2) Quick Break Attack Small Sided Game

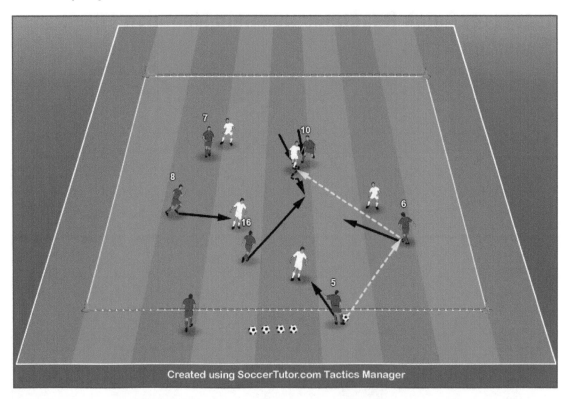

Created using SoccerTutor.com Tactics Manager

Objective

We work on quick reactions in the negative transition.

Description

In an area 40 x 40 yards, there is a 5v5 situation.

The red team retain possession with the help of the 2 outside players and aim to dribble the ball through the end line.

When the reds lose the ball, 1 of the outside players enters the area to help his teammates to regain the ball within 5 seconds. Once this is achieved, they should pass the ball to the other outside player in order to start a new attack.

The white team aim to win the ball and then retain possession for more than 5 seconds themselves (1 point), to dribble the ball through the end line (3 points) or both. If the ball goes out of play, the game restarts with the outside players in possession.

Only 1 outside player can enter the area during the negative transition. The outside players are limited to 1 touch throughout.

PROGRESSION

3. 5v5 (+2) Quick Break Attack Finishing Game

Created using SoccerTutor.com Tactics Manager

Objective
We work on quick reactions in the negative transition.

Description
2 teams play 5v6 inside an area 40 x 40 yards. There are also 2 red players outside this area who help

their teammates to retain possession.

The red players aim to dribble the ball through the end line and score within the 40 x 18 yard end zone. If possession is lost, the outside players enter the area to help their teammates win the ball within 5 seconds.

The whites aim to win the ball and dribble through the opposite end line or keep possession for more than 5 seconds (or both).

If the ball goes out of play, the coach passes a new ball to the red players. The white players are not allowed to follow their opponents into the end zone.

Coaching Points
1. There should be a safety player at all times.
2. Players need to be aware to always retain the team's balance.

PROGRESSION

4. Two Phase Negative Transition 11v11 Game

Created using SoccerTutor.com Tactics Manager

Objective

We work on quick reactions in the negative transition.

Description

2 teams play an 11v11 game in 2/3 of a pitch. The game has 2 phases.

PHASE 1: The red players try to carry out some set patterns of play when building up while the white players shift and act in a passive way defensively. During this set pattern, the ball is passed on purpose to 1 of the white players.

Once a white player has possession, the game changes to a normal competitive game with the red players aiming to win the ball back within 5 seconds and the whites trying to score. This phase can be run for 5-10 minutes.

PHASE 2: A regular game in which the red players aim to score and if they lose the ball, they should try to regain possession within 5 seconds. The whites try to win the ball and score themselves.

Coaching Points

1. The players need to be aware and have quick reactions after losing possession.

2. There should be a safety player at all times.

3. Players need to be aware to always retain the team's balance.

ATTACKING TACTICAL SITUATION 26

The Positive Transition

ANALYSIS

THE POSITIVE TRANSITION

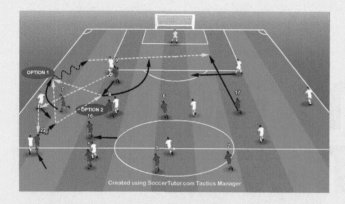

Situation 1

Regaining possession takes place near the sideline here. As No.22 wins the ball and leaves the opposition's wide midfielder behind him, a 2v1 situation is created.

No.7 moves towards the available space on the flank, while No.10 provides an available passing option. The ball can be passed either directly or through No.10 to No.7. Both ways the winger is free in space high up on the flank.

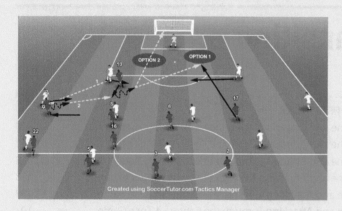

Situation 2

The ball is regained near the sideline again here.

As No.7 is in a 1v1 duel with the opposing full back, he directs the ball towards No.10 who provides a passing option towards the centre.

No.10 then has 2 passing options in the large gap left in the centre (one being to shoot at goal).

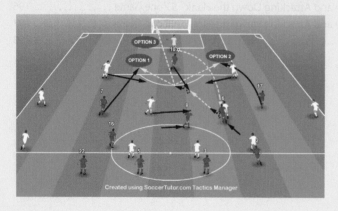

Situation 3

Barca regain the ball in the centre after the goalkeeper's long ball.

No.10 provides a passing option forward immediately.

He receives on the half turn and has 2 passing options towards the wingers who make runs inside and an option to shoot on goal himself.

ANALYSIS

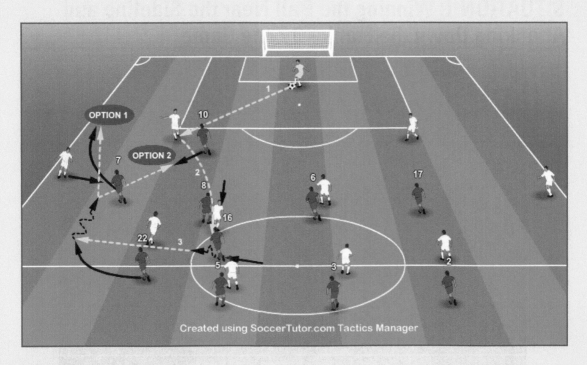

Created using SoccerTutor.com Tactics Manager

Situation 4

In this final example, Barcelona regain possession in the centre with the defensive midfielder, but he has no available passing option forward due to the opposition's pressure.

The full back (22) moves towards the sideline to provide width. As soon as No.22 receives from No.16, he moves quickly forward to take advantage of a potential numerical advantage (2v1).

Analysis

During the defensive phase, Barcelona looked to force the ball towards the sidelines where pressing was easier to apply. As soon as they regained possession, the players reacted quickly to move towards free space and provide passing options.

When Barca regained possession near the sidelines and there was superiority in numbers in their favour, the team would attack down that same flank. If there was not a numerical advantage, the team looked to move the ball towards the centre where the man in possession had many options.

When Barca regained possession in the centre, the new ball carrier had the opportunity to pass the ball forward and attack through the centre. In a situation like this, the wingers would make diagonal runs to receive.

If a forward pass could not be made, the ball was usually directed towards the sidelines. In order for this option to be available, the quick reaction of the full backs to create width was needed.

SESSION FOR THIS TACTICAL SITUATION
(9 PRACTICES)
SITUATION 1: Winning the Ball Near the Sideline and Attacking Down the Flank - 3 Zone Game

Created using SoccerTutor.com Tactics Manager

Objective

We work on the positive transition, winning the ball near the sidelines and attacking down the flank.

Description

In this small sided game, 2 teams play 6v5 with 1 extra neutral target player. The 2 white zones (12 x 30 yards) are exclusively for the full backs and the wingers, except for the red team's defensive midfielder (16) who can enter this area too. This means that the teams play 3v2 inside them.

The game starts with the coach passing to No.5 and No10's staring position is on the red cone (both must stay in the 6 x 30 yard middle zone). The coach passes the ball to white No.5 to start and the white team's aim is to find a way to pass the ball to the target player (green) in order to score a point.

The reds try to force the ball towards the white zones and win the ball by creating a numerical superiority around the ball zone. Then they attack through the same area with the aim to either dribble the ball through the red end line or receive beyond it. No.10 provides an additional passing option to make it easier to attack through the side zone. The offside rule is applied throughout.

Coaching Points

1. Players need to take advantage of the superiority in numbers out wide to block the passing options and win the ball.

2. Once they win the ball, players provide passing options immediately and attack the free space.

VARIATION

SITUATION 1: Winning the Ball Near the Sideline and Attacking Down the Flank - 4 Zone Game

Created using SoccerTutor.com Tactics Manager

Objective

We work on the positive transition, winning the ball near the sidelines and attacking down the flank.

Description

This small sided game is a variation of the previous drill with an additional end zone and 2 goalkeepers added. The rules are the same.

This time the goalkeeper makes the first pass towards the full backs inside the side zones. The 2 white players aim to find a way to pass the ball to their teammates and score past the goalkeeper.

The reds aim to create a numerical advantage (3v2) to win the ball and then attack through the same area by dribbling the ball through the red line or receiving beyond it and shooting (unopposed).

The reds have 6-8 seconds to work the ball into the end zone.

If the ball goes out of play, the game starts with the white goalkeeper in possession again.

SITUATION 2: Winning the Ball Near the Sideline and Attacking Through the Centre - 3 Zone Game

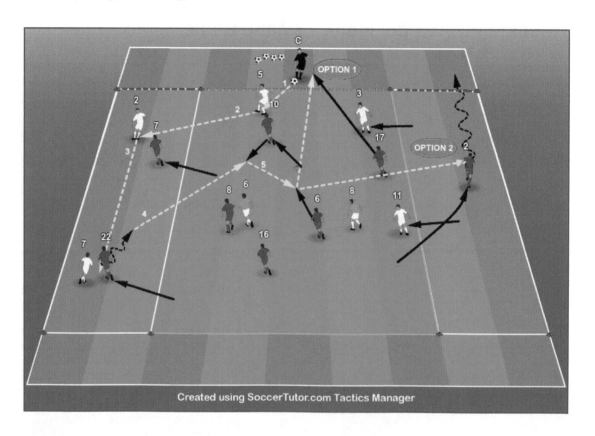

Created using SoccerTutor.com Tactics Manager

Objective

We work on the positive transition, winning the ball near the sideline and switching play.

Description

In an area 45 x 45 yards, we play an 8v7 small sided game. There are 2 side zones (10 x 45 yards) which are exclusively for the full backs and the wingers (2v2s). The offside rule is applied.

The game starts with the coach passing to No.5 and the white team look to pass the ball to 1 of the 2 target players (green) and score. If the ball is passed into the side zones, they must complete 2 passes before passing back to the middle.

The red players firstly seek to block the passes to the target players, then force the ball towards the white zones and regain possession there. As there is equality in numbers, as soon as possession is won, the players in the middle must provide passing options in order for the switch of play to be achieved.

The reds have 6-8 seconds to achieve their aim.

If the reds manage to dribble the ball or receive it beyond the red line, 2 points are scored. For the same through the blue line on the opposite side 1 point is scored.

VARIATION

SITUATION 2: Winning the Ball Near the Sideline and Attacking Through the Centre - 4 Zone Game

Created using SoccerTutor.com Tactics Manager

Objective

We work on the positive transition, winning the ball near the sideline and switching play.

Description

This is a variation of the previous drill. An end zone and 2 goalkeepers are added while the teams play with the same rules.

The reds again have 6-8 seconds available to achieve their aim and the offside rule is still applied.

The goalkeeper passes the ball and the white team aims to pass the ball to the target players (1 point). If the target players score, the goal counts double.

The reds seek to block the passes to the target players and move the ball wide to win poss ssion. If they win the ball and dribble/receive in the end zone, they can score unopposed. If they dribble through the red line, the goal counts double.

If the ball goes out of play, the game starts with the white goalkeeper.

SITUATION 3: Winning the Ball Near the Centre and Attacking Through the Centre - 3 Zone Game

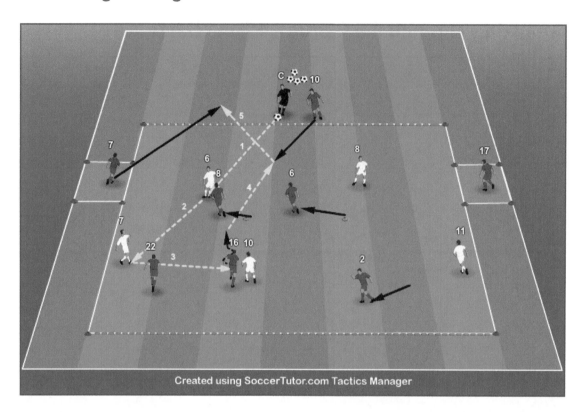

Created using SoccerTutor.com Tactics Manager

Objective

We work on the positive transition, winning the ball in the centre and attacking.

Description

In an area 35 x 45 yards, 2 teams play a 5v5 game. There are 3 additional red players (2 wingers are in 5 x 5 yard zones) outside the playing area ready to take part as soon possession as won.

The game starts with the coach passing to 1 of the white players. The red No.8 and No.6 start on the red cones. The white players aim to dribble or receive beyond the red line.

If the reds win possession, No.10 drops back inside the area to provide an extra passing option. The wingers are ready to use well timed diagonal runs to receive beyond the other red line.

The reds score a goal if they manage to dribble the ball through the red line or receive beyond it. The offside rule is applied. The red No.10 is not allowed to dribble the ball through the end line but can receive beyond it. The reds have 6-8 seconds to score once they win the ball.

Coaching Point

1. Quick reactions are needed to provide passing options (correct angles) when possession is won.
2. Players need to time their runs well and attack the free space.

VARIATION

SITUATION 3: Winning the Ball Near the Centre and Attacking Through the Centre - 4 Zone Game

Objective
We work on the positive transition by winning the ball in the centre and attacking.

Description
This small sided game is a variation of the previous drill. An end zone and 2 goalkeepers are added.

The same rules are used.

If the ball goes out of play, the game starts with the white team again with the white goalkeeper.

The reds still have 6-8 seconds to achieve their aim of getting beyond the red line.

As soon as the reds receive or dribble the ball through the red line, they can score in the end zone past the goalkeeper unopposed.

SITUATION 4: Winning the Ball Near the Centre and Attacking Down the Flank - 5 Zone Game

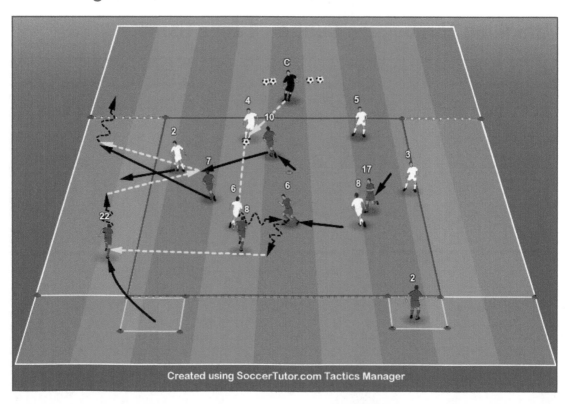

Created using SoccerTutor.com Tactics Manager

Objective
We work on the positive transition, winning the ball in the centre and then attacking down the flanks.

Description
We use an area 45 x 35 yards divided into 3 zones. 2 teams play 5v6 inside the central zone (25 x 25 yards) as the coach passes to one of the white players who try to keep possession. The aim for the whites is to dribble the ball through the end red line, or receive beyond it. The reds aim to prevent this.

The red No.10 starts on the red cone as shown. The full backs in the 5 x 5 yard yellow zones move quickly forward into the white side zones in order to receive and try to create a numerical advantage on the flank.

No.10 provides a passing option as the team aim to dribble the ball through the red line on the flank or receive beyond it. The offside rule is applied. Only the white full backs are allowed to enter the side zones. The reds have 6-8 seconds to score once they win the ball.

Coaching Points
1. Quick reactions are needed to provide passing options (correct angles) when possession is won.
2. Players need to time their runs well and attack the free space.

VARIATION

SITUATION 4: Winning the Ball Near the Centre and Attacking Down the Flank - 4 Zone Game

Created using SoccerTutor.com Tactics Manager

Objective

We work on the positive transition, winning the ball in the centre and then attacking down the flanks.

Description

This small sided game is a variation of the previous drill. An end zone and 2 goalkeepers are added. The teams play with the same rules.

The white goalkeeper starts by passing to one of his centre backs. The white team then try to score in the goal.

As soon as the reds win the ball, the full backs can move forward off the red cones to try and dribble the ball through the red line or receive beyond it (within 6-8 seconds). Once a player is in the end zone, they can shoot unopposed.

Only the white full backs can enter the side zones. When the ball goes out of play, the game starts again with the white goalkeeper in possession.

PROGRESSION

Positive Transition Game with 2 Side Zones

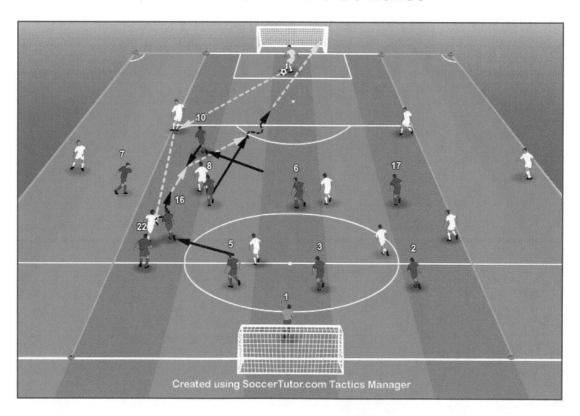

Created using SoccerTutor.com Tactics Manager

Objective

We work on the positive transition.

Description

2 teams play an 11v11 game. The white team build up play from the back (without using long passes) with the aim of scoring.

The red team apply pressure to win the ball back and must complete a successful counter attack within 8 seconds of gaining possession.

The blue zones are there to help the players read the tactical situation and move the ball towards the appropriate part of the field in order to develop the attacking move.

In case the ball goes out of play, the game restarts with the white team's goalkeeper.

Coaching Points

1. This practice should be done at a high tempo, with accurate passes, good communication and very quick finishing.
2. Players need to be able to read the tactical situation, have quick reactions when their team wins the ball and attack the free space (quick break attack).

DEFENDING

DEFENDING TACTICAL SITUATION 1

Chain Reaction of the Midfielders and the Forwards

ANALYSIS

CHAIN REACTION OF THE MIDFIELDERS AND THE FORWARDS

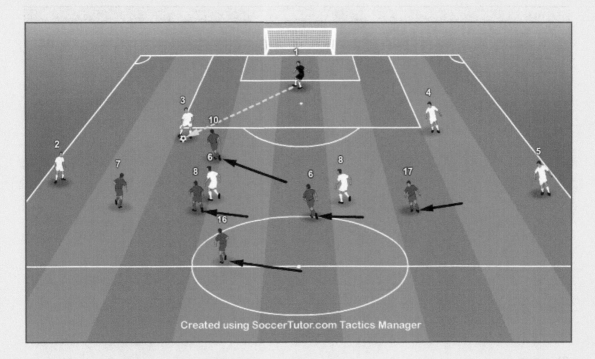

Created using SoccerTutor.com Tactics Manager

Analysis

During the defensive phase, Barcelona's forwards and midfielders would shift together in the form of a chain reaction. This horizontal shifting was made according to the position of the ball on the pitch and the players had to complete various tasks.

As can be seen in this example, the centre forward's (10) aim was to create a strong side and force the ball towards the sidelines.

The attacking midfielders (8 and 6) had to closely mark the opposing players who were near the ball zone, while the winger (7) had to block the potential forward passes and control the opposition full back's movements.

SESSION FOR THIS TACTICAL SITUATION
(3 PRACTICES)

1. Chain Reaction Pressing High Up the Pitch in Side Zones

Created using SoccerTutor.com Tactics Manager

Objective

We work on the chain reaction of the midfielders and the forwards to retain a compact formation.

Description

Using half a full pitch, set up 2 side zones as shown. The white players take up positions by the blue cones and pass the ball between themselves and the goalkeeper (retaining the ball).

The red players shift together according to the ball position. The whites players hold the ball for 5 seconds when they receive a pass, so the reds have time to shift across and then they can pass it to another player.

The shifting is synchronised and coordinated. Also, as soon as the ball reaches a white player inside one of the yellow side zones, the red players have to shift towards this side and leave the opposite side zone (weak side) unoccupied.

Leaving the weak side unoccupied allows the players to retain short distances between each other and keep a compact formation.

Coaching Points

1. The striker uses his body shape to prevent a switch of play and creates a strong side.
2. There should be short distances between the players during the pressing application.

PROGRESSION

2. Cohesion & Compactness in the Pressing Application

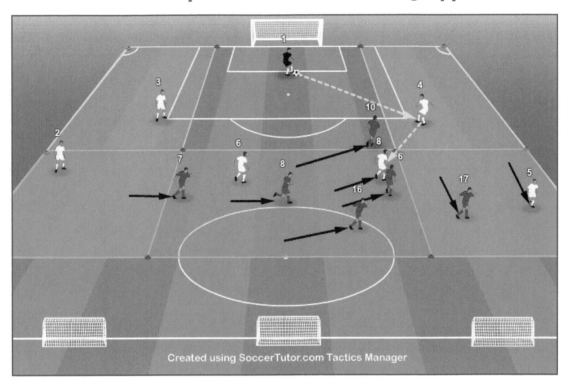

Created using SoccerTutor.com Tactics Manager

Objective

We develop our defending by maintaining the line's cohesion and compactness.

Description

We have a 6v6 (+1 goalkeeper) and there are 2 yellow side zones and a blue zone which stretches the full width of the pitch and covers a part of the yellow zones.

The white players try to score in 1 of the 3 mini goals and they must shoot within the blue area. All passes must be along the ground.

The red players defend as a compact unit, preventing the opposition from scoring within the blue area and if they win the ball, they can use a maximum of 4 passes to score past the goalkeeper.

When the white players pass the ball to a player inside one of the 2 yellow side zones, the red players should all shift towards this side and leave the opposite side zone (weak side) unoccupied.

This action helps them to maintain their cohesion and compactness.

Coaching Points

1. There should be short distances between the players during the pressing application.

2. There is a need to prevent the opposition from having available time and space in possession.

3. The potential forward passes must be blocked.

PROGRESSION

3. Cohesive Shifting Across to Press Near the Sidelines

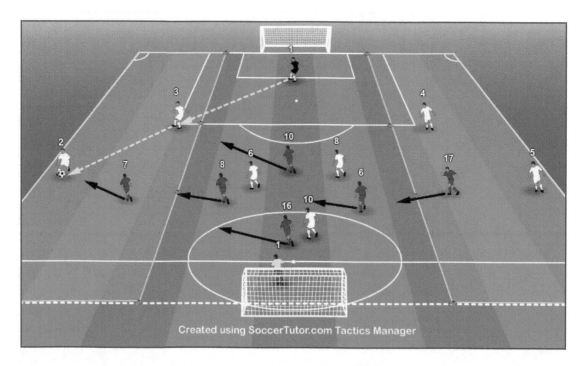

Created using SoccerTutor.com Tactics Manager

Objective

We develop our defending by maintaining the line's cohesion and compactness.

Description

Here we have an 8v7 small sided game with 2 side zones.

The white team start with a pass from their goalkeeper and aim to score, while the red team try to defend successfully and then launch a counter attack.

As soon as the white team passes the ball towards one of the 2 yellow side zones, the red players move across to leave the weak side unoccupied within 3 seconds. Otherwise the white team score a point.

The white team must keep their passes along the ground. The red team, after winning the ball, can only use a maximum of 4 passes for their counter attack as they try to score.

Coaching Points

1. The potential forward passes must be blocked.
2. The striker uses his body shape to prevent a switch of play and creates a strong side.
3. The wingers track the full backs' forward runs (when necessary).

DEFENDING TACTICAL SITUATION 2

Cohesion Between the Back 4 and the Defensive Midfielder

ANALYSIS

COHESION BETWEEN THE BACK 4 AND THE DEFENSIVE MIDFIELDER

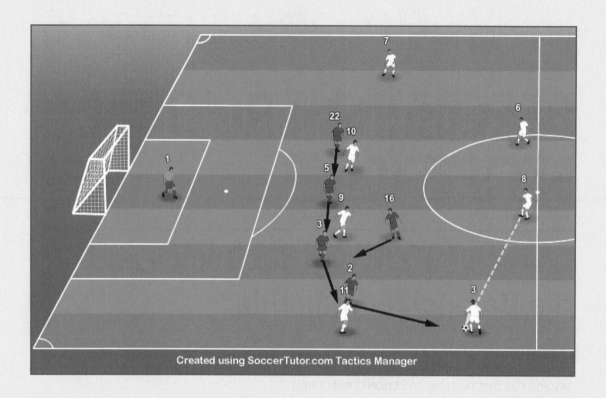

Created using SoccerTutor.com Tactics Manager

Analysis

The defensive midfielder (Busquets) played a very important role during the defensive phase of Barcelona. He would take up a position close to the 4 defenders in order to be able to fill in the possible gaps created when the players shift across.

In this example, the right back (2) takes advantage of the transmission phase and moves higher up to put pressure on the ball (white 3). The short distances between the players ensures quick and synchronised shifting.

This quick shift coincides with the quick switching in the marking of the opposition's players (red 2 to white 11, red 5 to white 9 and red 3 to white 11).

No.16 drops back in order for the team to retain a numerical advantage and be ready to fill any possible gap. If there were big distances between the defenders, No.16 would then drop into a central back's position.

SESSION FOR THIS TACTICAL SITUATION
(3 PRACTICES)
1. Synchronised Movement of the Defenders & the Def. Midfielder

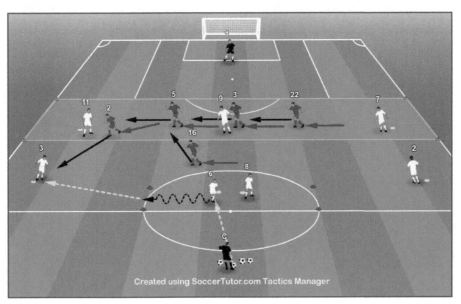

Created using SoccerTutor.com Tactics Manager

Objective

We train the chain reaction of the defenders and the defensive midfielder to apply immediate pressure on the ball and retain a compact formation, with a numerical superiority at the back.

Description

As shown we use half a pitch with a blue zone in which 4 defenders are positioned. The red defensive midfielder is outside the zone, but still close to the 4 defenders. The 2 white midfielders and 2 full backs are in positions by the yellow cones.

The coach passes the ball to 1 of the 2 white midfielders. This player receives and dribbles the ball towards the sideline, while the red players shift according to where the ball is. As soon as he dribbles it between the 2 blue cones, he passes towards the full back. The red full back takes advantage of the transmission phase and moves out of the zone to apply pressure.

No.16 moves into the zone to cover No.3 and retain balance. The ball is passed back to the coach and the players return to their staring positions.

During the second phase of the drill, the centre backs purposefully create large gaps between them in order for No.16 to fill in that position. The third situation is positioning No.16 higher up the pitch, so the defenders have to recognise the tactical situation and use offside tactics to counteract the attacking move. The first actions of the red players are indicated in the diagram by the blue arrows and the second by the black.

Coaching Points

1. There are short distances between the players and synchronised movements.
2. Good timing when putting pressure on the opposition's full back (prevent him from having time on the ball and do not allow him to scan the options around him).

PROGRESSION

2. 5v4 Chain Reaction Pressing Near the Sideline

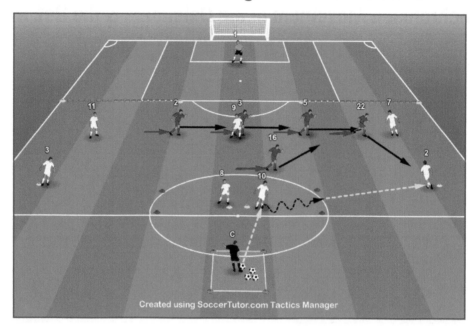

Created using SoccerTutor.com Tactics Manager

Objective

We train the chain reaction of the defenders and the defensive midfielder to apply heavy pressure on the ball during the first phase and create a superiority in numbers around the ball zone.

Description

For this practice, the red team use a 4-1 formation and the whites use a 4-3 formation. The coach determines the side where the attacking move will be developed by passing to 1 of the 2 midfielders.

The white players aim to dribble the ball through or receive it beyond the red line (offside rule is applied). If they succeed, they get 1 point and a further point if the player scores past the goalkeeper. If they are unable to break through the red team's defence on one side, they can try a second phase of attack using all the white players, but they have to score within 15 seconds.

The red's keep a compact formation to try and win the ball and then find a way to pass the ball to the coach. The red team can use a maximum of 4 passes after winning possession to achieve this. The first action of the red players is indicated by the blue arrows and the second by the black.

Progression

One more forward is added to the white team.

Coaching Points

1. In case the full backs realise that the timing is not good, they do not move forward, but instead wait for the defensive midfielder to put pressure on the player in possession.

2. There should be good communication between the players in order for the defensive midfielder to be aware of the tactical situation.

PROGRESSION

3. Closing Down the Opposition Full Backs Pressing Game

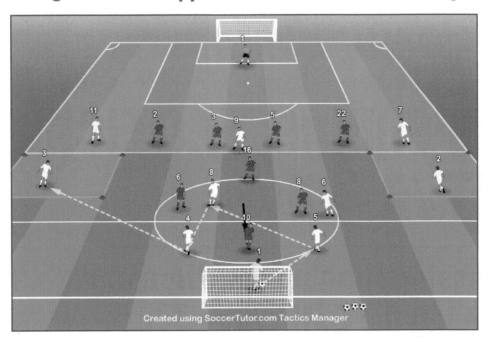

Created using SoccerTutor.com Tactics Manager

Objective

We train the chain reaction of the defenders and the defensive midfielder to apply heavy pressure on the ball during the first phase and create a superiority in numbers around the ball zone.

Description

The teams play 9v10 in an area that is divided into 2 zones; a high zone (yellow) and a low zone. Inside the low zone, there is a 4v4 with 2 additional blue areas (10 X 10 yards) for the 2 white full backs. Inside the high zone, there are 3 white forwards and 4 red defenders.

When the white team is in possession, the players stay in their respective positions. The white players in the low zone must complete at least 2 passes before they can pass the ball to the full back. The white team must attack through the full backs, who after receiving, must move or pass forward. When they do, the restrictions are removed and all players can move freely.

If the red full backs feel that the timing is not good, they do not move forward to contest the white full backs but all the defenders move back and give time for the attacking midfielders to close the man in possession down

The red team uses a chain reaction to defend and the key is in the timing. The defenders should be dropping back while the attacking midfielders should move to close the full backs down. When the red team win possession, they try to score by by using a maximum of 5 passes.

Coaching Points

1. There needs to be short distances between the players and synchronised movements.
2. Decision making is key, especially whether it is the right time for the full back to put pressure on the opposition's full back or not.

DEFENDING TACTICAL SITUATION 3

Pressing High up the Pitch and Forcing the Ball Wide

ANALYSIS

PRESSING HIGH UP THE PITCH AND FORCING THE BALL WIDE

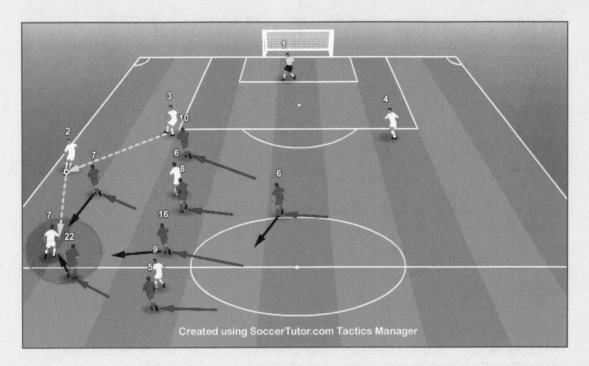

Analysis

One of the key elements of Barcelona pressing application was to force the ball towards the sidelines where the attempt to win the ball back was more likely to be successful.

In this example, the pressing that is being applied near the opposition's penalty area forces the ball towards the sideline as No.10 applies pressure by creating a strong side (his body shape prevents the ball carrier from switching play).

When the ball is near the sideline and all passing options are blocked, the switch of play is prevented and superiority in numbers is created (as No.16 moves close to the ball zone).

As soon as there is a pass to No.7, Barca are able to apply double marking. The first action is indicated by the blue arrow and the second by the black.

SESSION FOR THIS TACTICAL SITUATION
(5 PRACTICES)

1. Pressing the Ball Wide as a Compact Unit

Created using SoccerTutor.com Tactics Manager

Objective

We focus on the synchronisation of the players who all move as a compact unit. The chain reaction of the midfielders and the forwards are used to prevent forward passes and force the ball wide.

Description

We have 2 blue zones of 5 X 5 yards on the halfway line and near the sidelines for the white wingers and 2 small cone goals in the positions shown. The white players take up positions by the blue cones, except for the wingers who are positioned inside the blue zones.

As the white players pass the ball to each other (at the beginning in a slow tempo and then faster), the red players shift according to the ball position. They keep short distances between each other and try to block the potential forward passes from the centre backs towards the small goals.

The reds also force the ball wide and as soon as the winger receives the ball inside the blue area, he is double marked by No.7 and No.22. No.16 and No.8 move to ensure superiority in numbers around the ball.

The red players do not try to win the ball but they make sure that they take up the appropriate position in regards to the position of the ball. The white players continue to pass the ball around.

The first action is indicated by the blue arrows and the second by the black ones.

Coaching Point

Make sure there are short distances between the players.

PROGRESSION

2. Dynamic Pressing & Counter Attack Game

Created using SoccerTutor.com Tactics Manager

Objective

We work on the chain reaction of the midfielders and the forwards to prevent forward passes and force the ball wide.

Description

Here we play an 8v10 game. Inside the area there are 2 small cone goals and outside there is a red zone for the white forward.

The white team try to score 2 ways; either by passing through the small goals or by the ball to the striker who must control it within the red area. They are not allowed to use long passes.

The red team aim to block the potential forward passes, force the ball towards the sidelines and use double marking so it is easier for pressure to be applied and the pass towards the forward is more difficult to make.

When the red team wins possession, they counter attack using a maximum of 5 passes. If the ball goes out of play, the game restarts with the white goalkeeper.

Coaching Points

1. Make sure there are short distances between the players.

2. There is a need for synchronised movements for the pressing application to be fully successful.

PROGRESSION

3. Superiority in Numbers Around the Ball Zonal Game

Created using SoccerTutor.com Tactics Manager

Objective

We work on the chain reaction of the midfielders and the forwards to prevent forward passes and force the ball wide.

Description

2 teams play an 11 v 11 game in 2/3 of a full size pitch. There is a white zone (positioned as shown in the diagram) which is 35 x 35 yards.

The white team's goalkeeper starts and passes to one of the defenders. The white team has 3 aims in order to score a goal. They seek to complete more than 2 passes inside the white zone, to keep possession for more than 4 seconds inside the same area and finally, to score in the goal.

The red team tries to prevent these aims by forcing the ball wide, creating a numerical advantage near the sideline and double marking the ball carrier. If they win the ball, they counter attack using a maximum of 5 passes.

Coaching Points

1. Create superiority in numbers near the sideline and apply double marking.
2. There needs to be good communication and cohesion between the lines.

PROGRESSION

4. Pressing in 3 Stages Game with 4 Zones

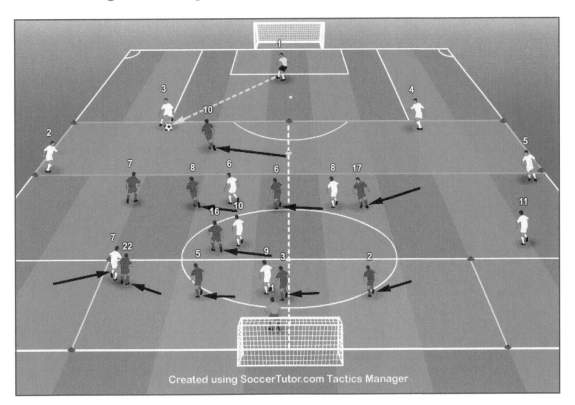

Created using SoccerTutor.com Tactics Manager

Objective

We work on the chain reaction of the midfielders and the forwards to prevent forward passes and force the ball wide.

Description

2 teams play an 11v11 game in 2/3 of a full size pitch. There is a blue area (10 x 50 yards) outside the white team's penalty area and a white zone in front of the red team's goal (35 x 35 yards).

The white team start the drill and have 3 aims; to pass the ball forward within the blue area to a player inside the white area, to switch the play towards the weak side of the red team (not via the goalkeeper) and to score. This means that the white team can get 3 points during 1 attack.

The red team want to prevent all of the above. They aim to force the ball towards the sideline, close the space by applying double marking and win possession.

If they win the ball, they can counter attack using a maximum of 5 passes.

The striker's (10) starting position is on the yellow cone and he is the one who applies pressure first to the white centre back (ball carrier). If the ball goes out of play, the game restarts with the white goalkeeper and the striker returns to his starting position.

VARIATION

5. Pressing in 3 Stages Game with 4 Zones (2)

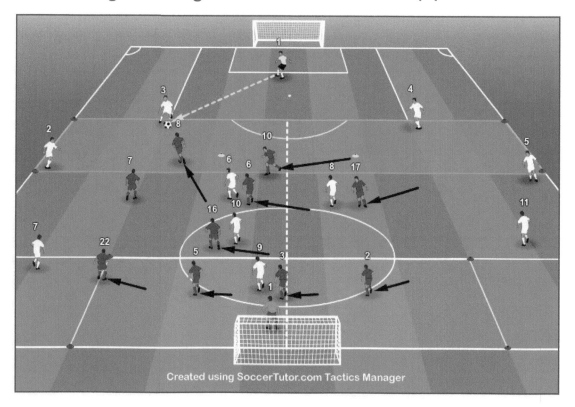

Created using SoccerTutor.com Tactics Manager

Objective

We work on the chain reaction of the midfielders and the forwards to prevent forward passes and force the ball wide.

Description

This is a variation of the previous game.

The white team has the same 3 aims again. The red team try to stop the white team, win the ball and counter attack.

The only difference here is that the attacking midfielder is the player who applies pressure on the ball first.

When the ball is in the white goalkeeper's possession, the striker takes up a position on 1 of the 2 yellow cones. The goalkeeper passes the ball towards the opposite side to where the striker is.

DEFENDING TACTICAL SITUATION 4

The Winger Puts Pressure on the Centre Back to Prevent the Pass Towards the Advanced Full Back

ANALYSIS

THE WINGER PUTS PRESSURE ON THE CENTRE BACK TO PREVENT THE PASS TOWARDS THE ADVANCED FULL BACK

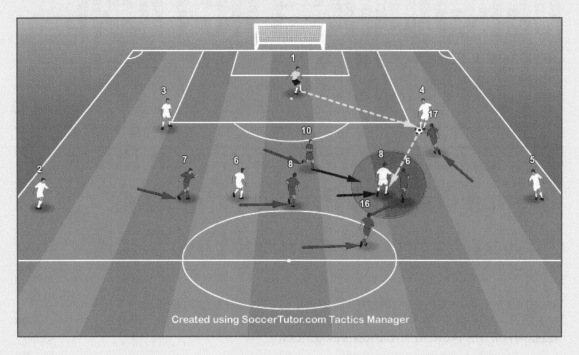

Created using SoccerTutor.com Tactics Manager

Analysis

During the pressing application near the opposition's penalty area, there were situations when the striker was far away from the strong side.

The team's aim was to prevent the opposition from having time on the ball and available space to move forward. So in some cases the winger was the player who applied pressure on the centre back in collaboration with the attacking midfielder. The winger would also use his positioning to prevent the pass towards his direct opponent (the opposing full back).

In this example, the goalkeeper passes to the centre back and Barca's striker (Messi - 10) is on the weak side.

As the full back (5) is in an advanced position and the new man in possession should be closed down, the winger (Pedro - 17) takes advantage of the transmission phase and puts pressure on white No.4. He also blocks a potential pass to No.5.

Xavi (6) moves to mark the white midfielder (8) in such a way that prevents him from receiving and passing to No.5. The first action is indicated by the blue arrows and the second by the black.

SESSION FOR THIS TACTICAL SITUATION
(3 PRACTICES)
1. Chain Reactions to Prevent Forward Passes

Created using SoccerTutor.com Tactics Manager

Objective

We work on the chain reaction of the midfielders and the forwards to prevent forward passes by applying pressure to the centre backs at the right time, denying them time and space.

Description

Using half a full size pitch, inside there are 2 blue zones (5 X 10 yards) for the white full backs and 1 white zone in the centre of the halfway line (5 X 35 yards) for the wingers. The red players are positioned by the blue cones, except for the striker who is positioned on 1 of the 2 yellow cones.

The white goalkeeper starts by passing the ball towards the opposite side to where the red striker (10) is. The red winger (17) applies pressure to the centre back in possession first.

The white team's aim is to pass the ball, either directly to the full backs, or through the wingers in order to score a goal. The red players want to prevent this. If there are no available passing options, the whites can pass back to their goalkeeper, the players get back to their starting positions and the drill starts again.

The white players are not allowed to move out of their zones and long passes are not allowed.

Coaching Points

1. Ensure the players take up the appropriate defensive positions.
2. There should be short distances between the players and synchronised movements.
3. The centre forward stays close to the midfielders in this exercise.

VARIATION

2. Preventing Forward Passes with a Numerical Superiority in the Central Zone

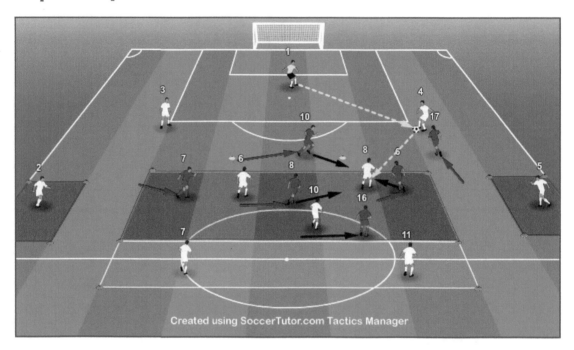

Created using SoccerTutor.com Tactics Manager

Objective

We work on the chain reaction of the midfielders and the forwards to prevent forward passes by applying pressure to the centre backs at the right time, denying them time and space.

Description

This is a variation of the previous practice and we add a 15 X 35 yard red zone in the centre. The white team builds up from the goalkeeper towards the opposite side to where the striker is positioned (on 1 of the yellow cones).

The winger is the one who puts pressure on the ball first. The white players have 2 aims; to pass the ball to the full backs (in the blue side zones) or to the wingers inside the white central zone. This can be done either by a direct pass or through the midfielders inside the red marked area.

The red team tries to prevent these aims, win the ball and counter attack using a maximum of 5 passes. The white players are not allowed to move out of the red central zone during the attacking phase or use long passes at any time.

Coaching Points

1. There should be short distances between the players to maintain cohesion.
2. The players should leave no time and space available for their opponents inside the red area.
3. The striker stays close to the midfielders in order to apply double marking as the ball is forced towards the centre.

PROGRESSION

3. Using Body Shape to Limit Passing Angles for the Centre Backs

Created using SoccerTutor.com Tactics Manager

Objective

We work on the chain reaction of the midfielders and the forwards to prevent forward passes by applying pressure to the centre backs at the right time, denying them time and space.

Description

We play a 9v10 small sided game which starts with the white goalkeeper. He passes the ball to the opposite side to where the red striker is positioned (on 1 of the 2 yellow cones). The first player to put pressure on the ball is the winger (17).

The white team aim to score and the red team defend. There are 2 blue zones (5 X 25 yards) near the sidelines for the 2 white full backs. If the ball is passed towards them, they can move forward with the ball freely as long as they are inside the area. However, when they move outside of it, they can then be put under pressure.

If the reds win the ball, they counter attack but can only use a maximum of 5 passes to score.

The white team are not allowed to use long passes. The full backs should be inside the blue areas during the attacking phase until they receive the ball.

Coaching Points

1. Players should take up the appropriate defensive positions.

2. The striker stays close to the midfielders in order apply double marking as the ball is forced towards the centre.

DEFENDING TACTICAL SITUATION 5

Defending Against a Centre Midfielder with Space to Create

ANALYSIS

DEFENDING AGAINST A CENTRE MIDFIELDER WITH SPACE TO CREATE

Analysis

When Barcelona had to deal with an opponent who had time and space in the centre of the field, the team's aim was to block the potential vertical and diagonal passes towards the forwards and to force the ball out wide.

In this example, the white midfielder receives the ball in the centre and moves forward as he has plenty of space to exploit.

Barcelona's midfielders move towards the centre and as there is an open ball situation, the defenders follow the attackers' forward movements.

Barca's aim remains to block the potential vertical and diagonal passes which are the most dangerous and force the ball towards the sidelines.

SESSION FOR THIS TACTICAL SITUATION
(3 PRACTICES)
1. Movements When Applying Pressure is not Possible

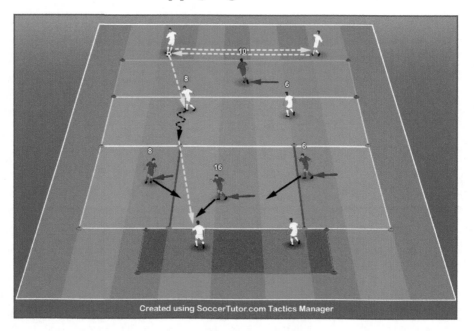

Created using SoccerTutor.com Tactics Manager

Objective

We train for when the pressing application was not possible in the centre of the pitch.

Description

In an area 30 x 40 yards, there are 4 different coloured zones. Inside the white area (15 X 30 yards) which is divided into 3 parts, there are 3 red midfielders (each one moves within his own area). The red striker is positioned inside the blue area (5 X 30 yards). Inside the yellow area (10 X 30 yards) there are 2 white midfielders and inside the red area (5 X 20 yards) there are 2 white forwards.

There are 2 white defenders outside the playing area.

The white defenders (outside) pass to each other at a low tempo and look to pass the ball to the midfielders. The white midfielders should receive on the half turn and find a passing lane to pass the ball to the white forwards inside the red area.

The red forward and the midfielders shift according to the ball position without moving out of their areas. As soon as one of the white midfielders receives the ball, the red midfielders can move freely in order to block the potential pass towards the red forwards. The first action is indicated by the blue arrows and the second by the black.

The white midfielders are limited to 2 touches (1 touch to turn and 1 to pass) and must make their pass from within the yellow zone.

Coaching Point

Players should be aware of the tactical situation and be taking up the appropriate positions in order to prevent the vertical and diagonal passes.

PROGRESSION

2. Movements When Applying Pressure is not Possible in the Centre

Objective

We train for when the pressing application was not possible in the centre of the pitch.

Description

We play a small sided game in 2/3 of a pitch with 3 marked out zones as shown. There are 2 white defenders outside of the blue area, a red forward inside the blue area and 2 white midfielders inside the red area. Inside the white area, there are 2 red centre backs and a defensive midfielder, together with 2 white forwards. During the first phase of the game, nobody else can move into this white area (3v2 situation).

The white centre backs start the game by passing the ball to each other. When they find the right moment they pass to the midfielders inside the red area. As soon as this happens, the game moves into the second phase (8v8) and everyone can move freely across zones. The man in possession tries to find a way to pass the ball (final pass) to a teammate inside the white area. The reds try to block this and force the ball out wide.

The white's aim is to score and the reds seek to defend successfully, win the ball and then complete 5 passes. The white team score a point if the midfielder manages to make a through pass into the white area and if they then score past the goalkeeper, the goal counts triple. The white centre backs do not take part in the second phase of the game.

Coaching Points

1. There should be synchronised movements, making sure to retain the cohesion.
2. Communication and short distances between the players is key.

PROGRESSION

3. Movements When Applying Pressure is not Possible in the Centre (2)

Created using SoccerTutor.com Tactics Manager

Objective

We train for when the pressing application was not possible in the centre.

Description

Inside the white low zone (25 yards long) there is a 6v3 situation. The white players retain possession and try to find a way to dribble the ball through the red line between the yellow cones and move into the yellow zone, where the red players are not allowed.

The red midfielders (8 and 6) during the first phase of the game stay outside of the red zone where there is a 3v2 situation. However, as soon as 1 white player moves into the yellow neutral area, the game moves into the second phase and everyone can then move freely across zones. They have 10 seconds to score from this point.

The white player in possession tries to find a way to make a final pass into the red area to score a point. If they then score past the goalkeeper, the goal counts triple.

The red players try to block the potential passes towards the players in the red area, force the ball wide or keep it near the sideline in order to more easily win the ball. If they win possession, they counter attack using a maximum of 5 passes. If the ball goes out of play, the game restarts with the white goalkeeper.

DEFENDING TACTICAL SITUATION 6

Cohesive Reactions When the Opposition Create Space Down the Flank to Attack

ANALYSIS

COHESIVE REACTIONS WHEN THE OPPOSITION CREATE SPACE DOWN THE FLANK TO ATTACK

Part 1

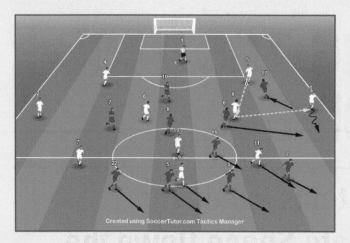

Analysis

In cases when Barca had to deal with an opponent who had time and space near the sidelines (open ball situation), the defenders dropped back to give time to the midfielders to shift and put pressure on the ball. They sought to keep the ball near the sideline in order for the attacking move to be limited.

When the man in possession was put under heavy pressure and could not pass the ball forward (closed ball situation), the defenders moved forward to restore the team's cohesion and reduce the depth of the attack.

In this example, the white team move the ball to the full back near the sideline and he has time and space on the ball. The defenders move back which gives time to the midfielders to be able to shift towards the sideline and close down the man in possession.

According to how advanced the full back's position is, a different player moves to close the ball carrier. In this specific situation, it is the attacking midfielder. If No.3 was in a more advanced position, it would have been the defensive midfielder.

As soon as Xavi (6) forces the white No.3 to turn towards his own goal (closed ball situation), the defenders move forward (indicated by the black arrows) to restore the team's cohesion.

Part 1

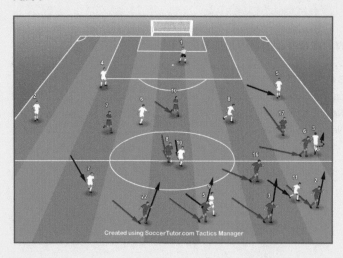

SESSION FOR THIS TACTICAL SITUATION
(3 PRACTICES)
1. Dealing With an Opponent Free in Space on the Flank

Created using SoccerTutor.com Tactics Manager

Objective

We work on defending when pressing is not possible near the sidelines.

Description

The coach starts this drill by passing the ball to 1 of the 2 white full backs. The full back who receives moves forward with the ball and the red players drop back in order to give time to their attacking midfielder to close down the man in possession.

As soon as the attacking midfielder closes down the ball carrier, the white full back (as he is unable to pass forward) passes back to one of the midfielders.

The red players take advantage of the transmission phase and move forward with synchronisation which also retains their cohesion.

The red players stop their forward movement as soon as the ball reaches the midfielder's feet. The ball is then passed back to the coach and the defenders move forward once again to restart the drill.

Coaching Points

1. Players need to read the tactical situation and use synchronised vertical movements.
2. There should be good communication between the players to maintain cohesion and balance.

PROGRESSION

2. Defending When Pressing is Not Possible Near the Sidelines

Objective

We work on defending when pressing is not possible near the sidelines.

Description

The teams play in 2/3 of a pitch with 2 red zones (15 X 10 yards) and 1 white zone (15 X 35 yards).

The white full backs and the red wingers are inside the red zones.

The coach starts the drill by passing the ball to 1 of the 2 white full backs, who the red wingers allow to dribble past them. The attacking midfielder on the strong side (or sometimes the defensive midfielder) closes down the man in possession. The ball carrier should be left with no options towards the centre (white area).

After the full back moves forward, all the players take part in the attack (8v9). The white team score a goal if the full back manages to pass into the white zone and if they then score past the goalkeeper in the same attacking move, the goal counts triple.

The red team try to block the potential passes into the white area, win the ball and complete 5 consecutive passes.

Coaching Point

Players should take up the appropriate position to block potential passes towards the inside.

PROGRESSION

3. Defending When Pressing is Not Possible Near the Sidelines (2)

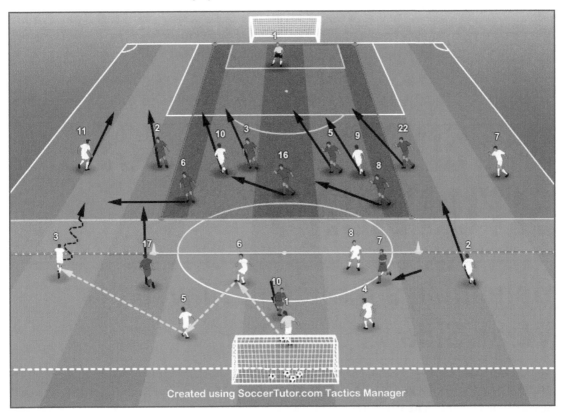

Created using SoccerTutor.com Tactics Manager

Objective

We work on defending when the pressing application is not possible near the sidelines.

Description

Inside the white zone (25 X 50 yards) there is a 6v3 situation. The white players retain possession and try to find a way to dribble the ball through the red line between the yellow cones on the sides and move into the neutral yellow zone. The red players are not allowed to enter the yellow zone.

The red midfielders (8 and 6) stay inside the red area (20 X 45 yards) during the first phase where there is a 5v2 situation. As soon as 1 white player moves into the yellow zone, the game moves into the second phase and everyone moves freely.

Second Phase: The man in possession tries to pass into the red zone (1 goal). If they then score past the goalkeeper in the same attacking move, the goal counts triple.

The red players try to block the potential passes towards the players in the red zone, force the ball wide (near the sidelines). If they win the ball, they counter attack using a maximum of 5 passes. If the ball goes out of play, the game restarts with the white goalkeeper.

DEFENDING TACTICAL SITUATION 7

Defending a Switch of Play to the Weak Side

ANALYSIS

DEFENDING A SWITCH OF PLAY TO THE WEAK SIDE

Part 1

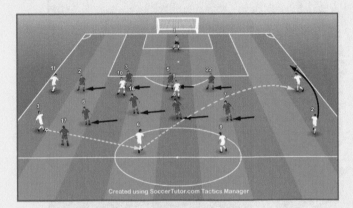

Part 2

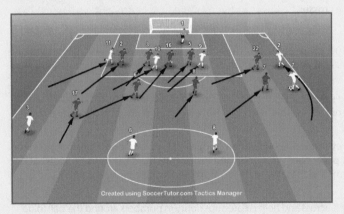

Analysis

When the play was switched towards Barcelona's weak side, the team had certain defensive reactions to deal with the situation.

The winger played a very important role as he controlled the forward movement of the opposition's full back and prevented the opposition from creating a numerical advantage on the flank.

The defensive midfielder sought to ensure the superiority in numbers inside the penalty area when the ball reached areas from where a cross could be made.

In this example, the winger (7) takes up a position in order to be able to control the white full back's forward runs.

As soon as there is a long ball towards the weak side and No.2 moves forward, Barca's No.7 follows his run.

Barca's No.22 and No.7 switch players and No.7 contests the man in possession, while No.22 takes over No.2's marking (who makes the overlapping run).

The rest of the players take up positions inside the box, helping to create a numerical advantage and get ready to neutralise a potential cross.

SESSION FOR THIS TACTICAL SITUATION
(3 PRACTICES)
1. 2v2 Play with Collective Defending on the Flanks

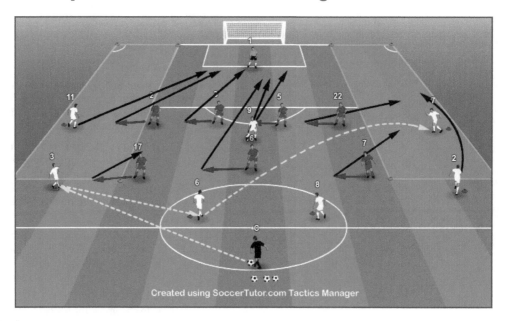

Created using SoccerTutor.com Tactics Manager

Objective

We work on preventing the opposition from creating a numerical advantage on the flanks, while taking up appropriate positions in the box to neutralise crosses.

Description

Using half a pitch, we have 2 blue zones of 10 X 35 yards on the flanks. The coach starts the drill by passing to one of the white team's full backs. The red players shift and take up positions according to the ball position (indicated by blue arrows).

When the defensive midfielder on the strong side receives the ball, he should play a long ball towards the red team's weak side. Their aim is to cross and score. When this happens, the red players shift across (indicated by the black arrows).

The red full back and the winger focus on preventing the opposition from creating a numerical advantage on the flank (inside the blue zones) by dealing with potential overlapping and inside runs from the opposing full back. The rest of the defenders and the defensive midfielder take up the appropriate positions inside the box and get ready for a potential cross.

As there is no time for the centre back (5) to shift across and help create superiority in numbers around the ball (blue area) on the weak side, he makes sure to take up an effective position inside the box (indicated by black arrow).

The coach asks for the red players on the flank to let their opponent cross the ball so the team can work on positioning and defending crosses.

Progression

Add an extra forward to the white team.

PROGRESSION

2. 3v3 Defending on the Flanks in a 3 Zone Dynamic Game

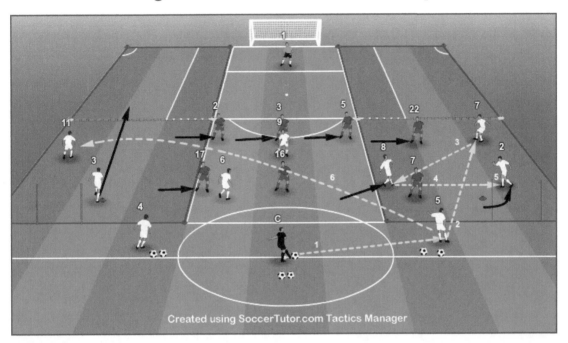

Created using SoccerTutor.com Tactics Manager

Objective

We work on preventing the opposition from creating a numerical advantage on the flanks, while taking up appropriate positions in the box to neutralise crosses.

Description

Using half a pitch, we divide the area into 3 equal sized zones. The coach starts by passing the ball to one of the white team's centre backs. As soon as they receive, the defensive midfielder (8) nearest to the strong side enters the blue side zone and the 2 teams play 3v2 inside this area. The full backs start on the blue cones.

At the same time, the red team's players have to leave the weak side unoccupied. As soon as all 3 white players have touched the ball or they manage to dribble the ball through the red line, the centre back (outside) plays a long pass with a new ball towards the other side and the second phase of the game begins.

Second Phase: The white players try to score with all zone restrictions now removed (all players can move freely) and the red players try to defend successfully on the weak side or neutralise the potential cross and then counter attack.

As soon as the red players win the ball in either of the 2 phases, all zone restrictions are removed and they can score in the 2 small goals near the sidelines (using a maximum of 5 passes in their attack).

PROGRESSION

3. Quick Collective Reactions: Defending on the Weak Side

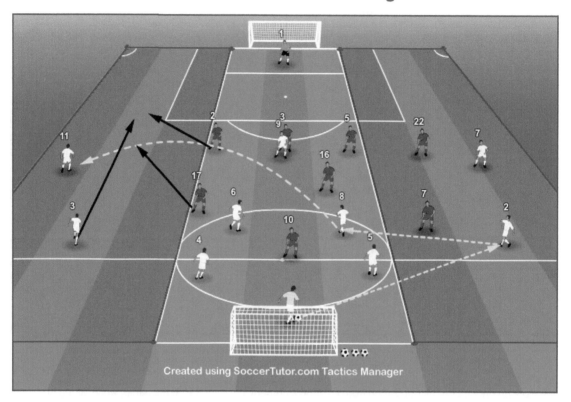

Created using SoccerTutor.com Tactics Manager

Objective

We work on preventing the opposition from creating a numerical advantage on the flanks, while taking up appropriate positions in the box to neutralise crosses.

Description

In this small sided game, the 2 teams play 9v10 in 3 equal sized zones. The red team plays with a 4-1-3 formation and the white team with a 4-2-3 formation.

The only restriction is that as soon as the white team moves the ball into 1 of the 2 blue side zones, the red players have to leave the opposite blue zone (weak side) within 3 seconds.

The white team look to take advantage of this by moving the ball quickly towards the weak side using long balls, quickly creating a numerical advantage.

Coaching Points

1. Short distances should be maintained between the players.
2. Good communication and synchronised movements are very important.
3. The wingers have to control the full backs' positioning.

DEFENDING TACTICAL SITUATION 8

Defending Near the Sideline and Close to the Penalty Area

ANALYSIS

DEFENDING NEAR THE SIDELINE AND CLOSE TO THE PENALTY AREA

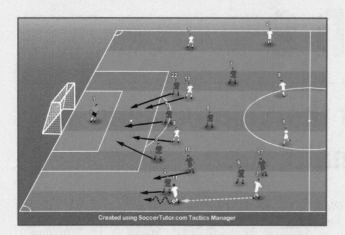

Situation 1

The opposing wide midfielder moves forward with the ball near the sideline.

The full back (2) contests him and the defensive midfielder (16) moves to provide support and superiority in numbers.

The rest of the defenders enter the box and take up the appropriate positions.

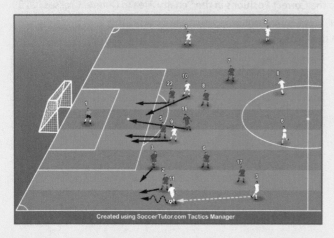

Situation 2

No.2 again moves to contest the man in possession. However, because No.16 is far away from the ball zone, the centre back (3) moves to provide support and superiority in numbers.

As the man in possession moves closer to the box, the rest of the defenders (together with the defensive midfielder) enter the box in order to avoid being outnumbered.

Analysis

In cases where the opposing team sought to attack through the flanks, Barcelona tried to create superiority in numbers around the ball zone. This was done either by the defensive midfielder's (Busquets) shifting close to the player in possession, or in cases when he was far from the ball zone, the centre back would shift to provide support.

SESSION FOR THIS TACTICAL SITUATION
(3 PRACTICES)
1. Creating a Numerical Advantage & Taking Up the Correct Positions in the Penalty Area to Defend Crosses

Part 1

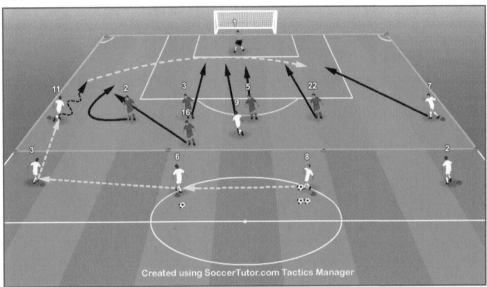

Part 2

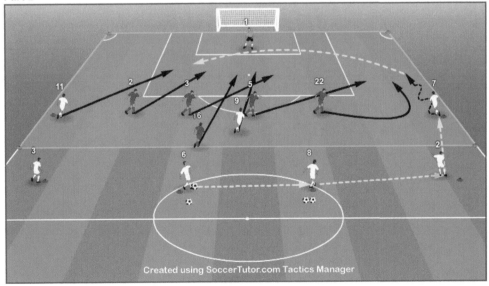

Objective

We work on creating superiority in numbers near the sideline as well as a numerical advantage in the penalty area.

Description

The white players pass the ball to each other outside the zone. As soon as the ball is passed to 1 of the 2 wingers inside the zone, the player in possession moves forward with the ball and crosses into the penalty area.

The red team's players shift according to the position of the ball, although they do not try to win the ball or prevent the winger from crossing.

The reds seek to create superiority in numbers near the sideline with the help of the defensive midfielder (situation 1) or with the help of the centre back (situation 2), as well as to defend the opposition's cross into the penalty area by taking up appropriate positions and retaining a numerical advantage inside the box.

Coaching Points

1. The white team's passes must be short and and in sequence so that the red players have time to shift towards the strong side.

2. As the defensive midfielder is near the strong side, he is the one who creates superiority in numbers near the sideline.

PROGRESSION

2. Preventing the Cross on the Flank by Creating a 2v1 Advantage

Created using SoccerTutor.com Tactics Manager

Objective

We work on creating superiority in numbers near the sideline as well as a numerical advantage in the penalty area.

Description

Using half a pitch, in this small sided game we play 5v5 + 2 outside players, with 2 yellow zones near the sidelines and a blue zone across the width of the pitch.

The white team aim to move the ball (with the help of the 2 outside players) into the yellow zones near the sidelines and cross the ball into the box. Long passes are not allowed during the attacking phase of the white team.

The red team's full backs follow their direct opponent's movement into the yellow zones and try to prevent them from crossing the ball. However, they are not allowed to win the ball unless there is a second red player inside the yellow area. The red team also has to defend successfully against a potential cross.

If the reds win the ball, they try to pass it to the coach who is positioned inside the red area using a maximum of 4 passes.

Coaching Point

Communication is essential between the players in one specific instance. The player who is about to create superiority in numbers inside the yellow zone has to let his teammate know when he has entered the yellow zone, so he knows he is then able to tackle the opponent.

PROGRESSION

3. Creating a Numerical Advantage High Up on the Flank to Block Crosses

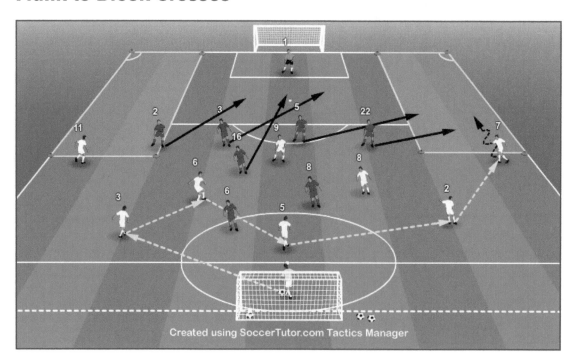

Created using SoccerTutor.com Tactics Manager

Objective

We work on creating superiority in numbers near the sideline as well as a numerical advantage in the penalty area.

Description

In an area slightly larger than half a pitch, 2 teams 8v9. The red team use a 4-1-2 formation and the white use a 3-2-3 formation. There are 2 yellow zones near the sidelines.

The white team try to develop their attacking play through the flanks (yellow zones) and get crosses into the box. They are not allowed to use long balls.

The red team aim to create superiority in numbers (inside the yellow zones and inside the penalty area) in order to win the ball or neutralise a potential cross.

If the reds win the ball, they have to counter attack using a maximum of 5 passes.

Coaching Points

1. There should be short distances between the players and synchronised movements.
2. Express the importance of good communication between the players.

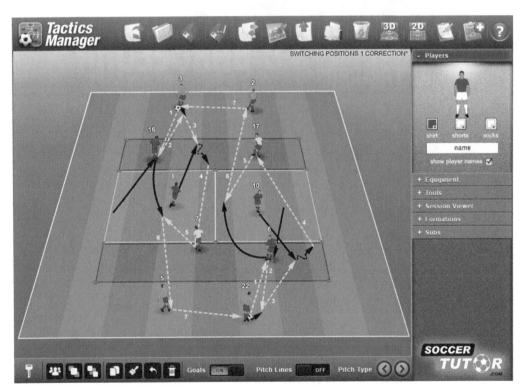

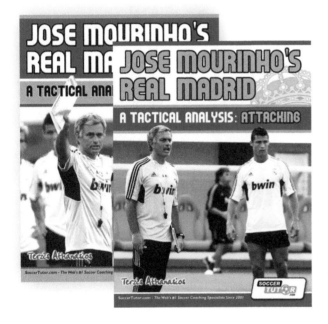